The Intuitive Arts

on

MONEY

The Intuitive Arts
on
MONEY

Arlene Tognetti and Katherine A. Gleason

ALPHA
A member of Penguin Group (USA) Inc.

International Standard Book Number: 1-59257-107-7
Library of Congress Catalog Card Number: 2003111788

05   04   03   8   7   6   5   4   3   2   1

Interpretation of the printing code: The rightmost number of the first series of numbers is the year of the book's printing; the rightmost number of the second series of numbers is the number of the book's printing. For example, a printing code of 03-1 shows that the first printing occurred in 2003.

Printed in the United States of America

Most Alpha books are available at special quantity discounts for bulk purchases for sales promotions, premiums, fund-raising, or educational use. Special books, or book excerpts, can also be created to fit specific needs.

For details, write: Special Markets, Alpha Books, 375 Hudson Street, New York, NY 10014.

Publisher: Marie Butler-Knight
Product Manager: Phil Kitchel
Senior Managing Editor: Jennifer Chisholm
Senior Acquisitions Editor: Randy Ladenheim-Gil
Book Producer: Lee Ann Chearney/Amaranth Illuminare
Development Editor: Lynn Northrup
Copy Editor: Keith Cline
Technical Editor: Reba Jean Cain
Cover Designer: Charis Santillie
Book Designer: Trina Wurst
Creative Director: Robin Lasek
Layout/Proofreading: Angela Calvert, John Etchison

Contents

Appendixes

Introduction

Claim your brightest destiny and fulfill your own essential nature.

More than ever, we are searching for an inner awareness that brings outer confidence, joy, and direction. *The Intuitive Arts* series, with volumes on Money, Family, Health, Love, and Work, gives readers looking for answers to questions of daily living tools from the esoteric arts that will help them look deeply, see, and make real changes affecting their futures. Curious querents are presented in each problem-solving volume with exercises in the Intuitive Arts of Astrology, Tarot, and Psychic Intuition that examine, instruct, illuminate, and guide. In essence, you get three books for one—but also so much more!

An understanding of the interplay of the Intuitive Arts of Astrology, Tarot, and Psychic Intuition is something most people gain slowly over time, or with the aid of a professional Intuitive Arts practitioner who already has the knowledge to give in-depth readings that link the arts together.

In *The Intuitive Arts* series, expert author Arlene Tognetti shares her deep knowing of the arts of Astrology, Tarot, and Psychic Intuition to give you the best opportunity to work out solutions to life's problems and challenges. With the benefit of the sophisticated relationships between the arts, Arlene reveals, chapter by chapter, the issues that matter to you. By combining the Intuitive Arts in the exercises of each chapter, you'll gain insights that link the arts together—how, for example, the Tarot's Elemental reactions deepen insights into your astrological Elemental Abundance Signature. Or what Psychic Intuition reveals about how Astrology's Nodes ☊ ☋ hold your financial karmic lessons—past, present, and future.

Arlene Tognetti and New Age book producer Lee Ann Chearney at Amaranth Illuminare created this series for Alpha Books to respond to the public's growing fascination with all things spiritual. People (like you!) want to know how they can use the Intuitive Arts to solve everyday challenges, plan for the future, and live in the present, with hands-on advice and techniques that will make things better for them. We want to help you improve the issues surrounding your unique life situation by providing a multi-art approach that gives you multiple pathways to personal growth and answers your questions about money, family, health and well-being, love, and work.

Using Tarot's Major and Minor Arcana cards and spreads, Astrology's birth charts and aspect grids, sign, planets, and houses, and Psychic Intuition's meditations, affirmations, and inner knowing exercises, the innovative *Intuitive Arts* series provides a truly interactive, solution-oriented, positive message that enriches a personal synergy of mind, body, and spirit!

Read on to further your knowledge and understanding of how the Intuitive Arts work together to reveal deep insights. In this series volume, *The Intuitive Arts on Money,* learn how Astrology, the Tarot, and Psychic Intuition reveal your future wealth—both material and spiritual!

Are *you* ready for abundance?

chapter 1

Money, Money, Money, Money

Meet the Intuitive Arts
Psychic Intuition and the dollar
The Tarot: Picture your abundance
Astrology: Pennies from heaven?
Planetary cycles and money
What is money?
Your personal abundance

Money, in one form or another, seems to be the topic that is on everyone's mind. We read about it, worry about it, spend it, and try to save it. We watch our bank accounts shrink and grow. We feel money underpinning almost all of our daily activities. If you ask professionals in the field of the Intuitive Arts what people want to know about most, money and finances are among the topics at the top of the list. That's why in this book we've merged money and the Intuitive Arts. Now, this might not be the type of corporate merger that makes headlines, but it can help you turn a profit. But before we show you how you can work toward the abundant life you've always wanted, we introduce you to money through the lens of the Intuitive Arts of Astrology, Tarot, and Psychic Intuition.

What Are the Intuitive Arts?

Astrology, Tarot, and Psychic Intuition, all branches of the Intuitive Arts, are powerful tools that can allow you to get in touch with forces inside yourself. They also provide a window through which you can view the energies that surround you and help to define your experiences. Many people think of Astrology, Tarot, and Psychic

Intuition as metaphors for their inner selves and the lives they lead. With a little knowledge, which we provide throughout this book, you can use these Intuitive Arts to better understand yourself, your desires, and your relationship to your own abundance. All you need (besides a copy of this book) are a few simple tools, which we describe in a moment; a pen; and a notebook in which to record what you learn about you.

Astrology is the study of the positions and motions of the heavenly bodies with an eye to how their locations and movements affect life on Earth. The behavior of a planet in the sky indicates a certain energy that will have a manifestation in your life or surroundings. The astrological configurations formed by the planets in the sky show what is happening here on Earth, or as astrologers like to say, "As above, so below."

An astrologer uses your birth chart, a map of the sky at the time you were born, to analyze the patterns and energies that form a part of your unique personality. You can think of your birth chart as a snapshot of you at birth. Or you can think of it as a metaphor for your personality, complete with your talents and your habits—both good and bad. Although we provide examples of birth charts throughout this book, the focus here is really on you. So you will want to have a copy of your own birth chart to examine and analyze as you read.

If you do not already have a copy of your birth chart, you should have one made. To do this, you need to provide an astrologer with the date—month, day, and year; the time; and place of your birth. If you do not know the time you were born, you might be able to get this information from your birth certificate. If your birth certificate does not have a time on it, you might be able to obtain this information from the hall of records in the town where you were born. But don't worry—if you can't determine your time of birth, an astrologer can still draw up a chart for you. When the time of birth is unknown, astrologers use noon as the birth time because noon is the middle of the day.

You have a number of different choices when it comes to ordering your birth chart—you can get one online or from your local New Age shop, or you can seek an astrologer in your area by word of mouth. There's more information about how to go about ordering your chart in Appendix A. Arlene, co-author of this book, used the computer software program Solar Fire 5 by Astrolabe, Inc., to generate the birth charts we've adapted as examples throughout this book. Charts are cast using the Geocentric view, Tropical Zodiac, Placidus house system, and True Node because these are the most common in modern Western Astrology. To use your birth chart with this book, you need to be sure to specify these parameters when generating your own astrological birth chart.

We imagine that you have picked up this book because you want more money in your life. Or you feel that you should be making more money. Because you are interested in wealth, take a look at what the chart of a wealthy person looks like.

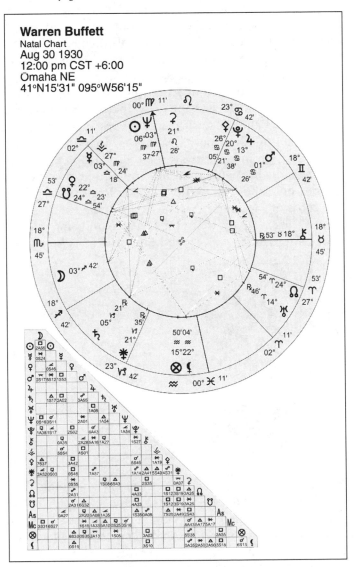

Warren Buffett's astrological birth chart and aspect grid.

3

Warren Buffett is one of the richest men in the world. Even if you don't yet understand what it all means, spend a little time right now to look at Buffett's chart. You can think of this chart as a metaphorical baby picture of Warren himself. Because we have not been able to pin point the exact moment that Warren appeared in the world, this chart is a noon chart, meaning that Arlene used noon as Warren's time of birth. When examining a noon chart, keep in mind the Moon ☽ could have been in a different sign at the actual time of birth. If your Psychic Intuition kicks in while you are looking at this image, make some notes about what it is telling you. Later in this chapter, we spend some more time with Warren and his astrological energies.

Another thing that you need in your journey through this book is a deck of Tarot cards. Tarot cards provide another metaphor for the energies inside of you and those surrounding you. A Tarot deck consists of 78 cards, all of which bear images that function as potent symbols to your intuitive mind. These symbols can help you to see below the surface of what is happening around you and help you understand financial events, both those caused by outside forces and those initiated by you. The cards of the Major Arcana, a grouping of 22 cards in the Tarot deck, describe the path that you as a human being take through your life. Take a look at the Fool, the Major Arcana's first card.

The Fool is the first card in Tarot's Major Arcana.

The Fool looks like a pretty happy guy, don't you think? The Fool may be a fool (and we all are to a certain extent), but, at the same time, he represents someone who is willing to learn—a beginner, and in that respect we think he's pretty smart. The Fool is all about beginnings and the start of new things. Because we all have to start somewhere, let's start with him and allow his open-mindedness and joy to color the journey you are about to take through this book. You'll find illustrations depicting all the other cards at the back of this book, but you will want to have your own deck of Tarot cards, too. You can find a Tarot deck at your local metaphysical or New Age shop. Some of the chain bookstores carry them, too. The deck we use in this book is the popular Universal Waite deck published by U.S. Games Systems, Inc.

To access your Psychic Intuition, all you need is yourself and a quiet moment. Your Psychic Intuition is that voice inside you that always knows the right thing to do. It's your sixth sense that gives you hunches or sudden flashes of insight. Your Psychic Intuition is what gives you your ability to know who is calling on the phone before you pick up (and without checking your caller ID box). Your Psychic Intuition is also a key that you will use to unlock the meaning of the Tarot cards when you lay out a financial spread, and it will aid you in interpreting the fiscal implications of your birth chart. Because you don't need any special equipment to employ this most special skill, we're going to have you try a Psychic Intuition exercise right now.

By George!

Find a little quiet time to yourself. Keep your notebook nearby and take a $1 bill out of your wallet. Examine the bill on both sides. Notice George Washington's expression, the little leaves that wrap around the numerals in the top corners, and the Department of the Treasury seal with its balanced scales and key. On the back side, see the two sides of the Great Seal of the United States—the pyramid topped with a floating eye and the bald eagle with his arrows and shield.

Once you feel that you have thoroughly examined this dollar bill, keep the bill in your hand and close your eyes. Take a few breaths to relax. Shake out your shoulders if they feel tense. When you are settled, focus on the overall feeling that you get from the dollar. Make sure that you keep breathing as you do so.

Spend a few minutes with your eyes closed, exploring what comes up for you. Your feelings may be connected to an image or to a story from your life. Your feelings may have words attached to them, but they may not. Whatever form your Psychic Intuition uses, it is communicating valuable information to you. Now, imagine that George Washington has something to say to you. You see his lips move. You hear his voice. Once you feel that you have received the message that George and your intuition are sending, open your eyes and record what you have heard.

Take notes on what George has to say and also on the feelings that came up for you throughout your contemplation of the dollar bill. If there is a story connected with your feelings, you may want to take the time to write it out and see what it can tell you about your present-day feeling about money and your sense of abundance.

If you enjoyed this last exercise and you already have a deck of Tarot cards, try one more thing. This exercise will help you become familiar with the cards if they are new to you, and it will provide further insight into your relationship with George.

A Fool and His Friends

You've already met the Fool earlier in this chapter. Now you are going to have the opportunity to meet the rest of the cards from the Tarot. This exercise is best done on a large table or on the floor because you will want room to spread out. Keep your dollar bill and George visible and fan out all your Tarot cards face up so that you can see their images. Look through all of the images on all of the cards. Once you have a good feel for the cards, spend some time looking at your dollar bill again. Look George Washington in the eye. When you feel you've got the energy of the dollar bill, pick a Tarot card that you feel represents the dollar bill and its energy. The card you choose does not have to resemble the dollar bill physically, but it may. Try to let yourself feel which card is most like the dollar on an energetic level.

When Arlene tried this, she liked the 10 of Cups and the 7 of Pentacles, but she was also drawn to the Queen of Pentacles and the Knight of Wands because of the pyramids in the background.

Using her Psychic Intuition, Arlene chose these cards as having similar energy to the dollar bill.

Katherine, your other co-author, chose the King of Cups, whose face does seem a lot like George's face, and Temperance from the Major Arcana. She felt that George had the same kind of relaxed vibe that the angel on the Temperance card displays, whereas the King of Cups just might be a little wary of the future.

Using her Psychic Intuition, Katherine chose these cards as having similar energy to the dollar bill.

Now that you've had an experiential introduction to the Tarot, let's look at this intuitive art form more closely.

Tarot: A Picture of Your Abundance

People have used Tarot cards for centuries. A few museums even have decks that date back as far as the 1400s. Around 1900, a man named A. E. Waite hired Pamela Coleman Smith to draw the images for the cards on the Universal Waite deck we use in this book. If you have your own copy of the Universal Waite deck, you can see her intertwined initials at the lower-right corner of each card. There are many other styles of Tarot cards available. Although their images and colors may differ somewhat, they are all based on the same elements of human experience. As we have already noted, there are 78 cards in a Tarot deck. Of these, 22 form the Major Arcana, each of which represents a major signpost on the karmic road of your life; and 56 cards make up the Minor Arcana. The cards of the Minor Arcana are a lot like regular playing cards. They even have four suits, but instead of Clubs, Hearts, Spades, and Diamonds, the Tarot has Wands, Cups, Swords, and Pentacles. Wands is the Tarot suit of enterprise and creativity, Cups is the suit of emotion and love, Swords is the suit of action and power, and Pentacles (you guessed it!) is the suit of money and abundance. The Minor Arcana cards are "everyday" cards and show your free-will decisions.

Psychiatrist Carl Gustav Jung (1875–1961) studied the Tarot and found that the pictures on the cards illustrate timeless archetypes of human transformation. Archetypes such as those represented in the Tarot appear in all the cultures of humankind. Thus, the Tarot is able to help you connect to the collective unconscious—the pool of myths and symbols that are universal to humankind. As you have already seen, you can use the Tarot as a way of describing a sense you have gotten from your Psychic Intuition. You can also use an image from the Tarot as a focus for meditation or contemplation as you did with George on the dollar bill. And, of course, you can use the cards in spreads, special patterns of cards that will "tell" your future.

But are the cards really able to foretell your financial future? Tarot is a tool that can show you possibilities. It can also be a forum for self-exploration. The cards themselves do not know anything and cannot predict your future or the future of your bank account. No matter what the cards say, you still have free will, which you must use to determine your own fate.

When you execute your free will to use Tarot cards in a spread to gain more information about yourself or the possibilities that surround you, you usually shuffle them and, without looking at them first, lay them down on the table. Then you look at the spread of cards to see which cards have come up. The cards can appear upright or reversed—upside down. A card in the reversed position is not considered negative, and it does not indicate the opposite of the card when it is upright. Reversed cards can indicate ambivalence, delays, false starts, indecision, or frustration. The cards, when reversed, may be asking you to rethink or reconsider. As you know, the Fool indicates a new beginning or a fresh start. The Fool R (the "R" stands for reversed) says that your path may have delays or present more of a challenge than you had anticipated.

Some cards, such as the Devil, are actually more positive when reversed. The Devil represents bondage to an obsession, an addiction, or to material goods. The Devil R signifies a breaking of those obsessive bonds and stepping away from fear. Which Devil would you choose to describe yourself and your relationship to your finances right now?

Upright, the Fool speaks of fresh starts and new beginnings. Reversed, the card describes delays or challenges.

Upright, the Devil speaks of materialism or bondage to an obsession. Reversed, the card describes breaking the chains of obsession and moving toward freedom.

Time for Tarot

When using the Tarot for your financial forecasting, in addition to paying attention to whether a card is reversed or upright, you want to look at the number on the card's face and the status of your court cards. The cards of each suit in the Minor Arcana are numbered 1 to 10, followed by a Page, a Knight, a Queen, and a King. (So each suit has one more court card than a deck of regular playing cards does.) The number or level of the cards in a reading indicate when the financial events you have asked about will come to pass. So Tarot has its own built-in timing system! Here's a chart of card numbers along with the court personalities and how they relate to event timing.

Tarot Cards	Tarot Timing
Ace through 10	1 to 10 days, weeks, or months (depending on the card, of course)
Page	11 days, weeks, or months
Knight	12 days, weeks, or months
Queen and King	Unknown time—it's up to you!

Here's another tip that you can use when asking the cards about the future of your money. In addition to the number or court card status, each Tarot suit—Wands, Cups, Swords, and Pentacles—describes a time frame.

Tarot Suits	Tarot Suit Timing
Wands	Days to weeks
Cups	Weeks to months
Swords	Hours to within a few days
Pentacles	Months to years

The numbers on each card also have metaphysical significance. According to Numerology, the esoteric study of numbers and their energies, each number has its own vibration and meaning. Numerology uses the numbers 1 through 9. Any two-digit number is reduced by adding the digits together. For example, the number 13 in numerology is seen as 1 + 3 = 4. So the number 13 resonates to the number 4. Find the meaning for 4 on the table below, and make sure to refer to this chart when filling in your own numerological balance sheet.

Number	Key Terms
1	Drive and determination
2	Balance and union
3	Creative enthusiasm
4	Practical planning
5	Impulsive spontaneity
6	Nurturing concern
7	Serene contemplation
8	Powerful achievement
9	Spiritual completion

The cards of the Major Arcana also bear significant numbers. They are numbered starting with 0 for the Fool and ending with 22 on the World card, the sign of attainment and completion. The numbers on the cards of the Major Arcana can further illuminate the timing of events. Or you can see the numbers as resonating to the energy of the cards and further expanding on the card's symbolic meaning. Either way, you'll want to pay attention to the numbers and their resonances for each card in your financial spread.

Astrology and You

Maybe you already know something about Astrology. Perhaps you check your horoscope regularly in a newspaper or magazine, in which case you know your Sun ☉ sign, which the general public often refers to as your Zodiac sign, or just your sign. If you don't already know your Sun sign, take a look at the following chart. Locate your birth date on the Zodiac wheel and find the Sun sign that coincides with the date of your birth.

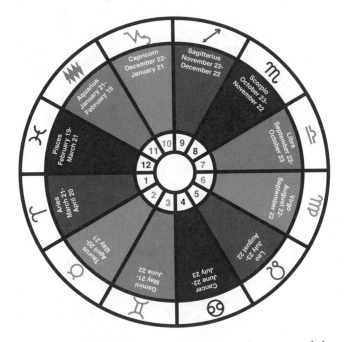

To find your Sun ☉ sign, simply note the name of the astrological sign that correlates to your birth date.

Each sign of the Zodiac is named after a constellation of stars in the sky. From the vantage point of the Earth, the Sun ☉ appears to travel through each constellation and its area. The Sun is said to be "in" the given sign at that time, and individuals born at that time are said to have that Sun sign. For example, if you were born in February and are an Aquarius ♒ (and Arlene is), the Sun ☉ at the time of your birth appeared to be in the area of the sky named for the constellation Aquarius. People born under the same Sun sign are said to share some characteristics. Find your Sun sign in the following table and see if the keywords for your sign illuminate some facets of your personality and your approach to your finances.

Astro Sign	Symbol	Dates	Keywords
Aries	♈	March 21 to April 20	Energetic, take-charge, pioneering
Taurus	♉	April 20 to May 21	Sensual, grounded, down-to-earth
Gemini	♊	May 21 to June 22	Resourceful, quick-witted, mercurial
Cancer	♋	June 22 to July 23	Empathetic, nurturing, emotional
Leo	♌	July 23 to August 22	Charismatic, fun-loving, confident
Virgo	♍	August 22 to September 22	Resourceful, practical, analyzing
Libra	♎	September 22 to October 23	Principled, balanced, harmonious
Scorpio	♏	October 23 to November 22	Passionate, powerful, profound
Sagittarius	♐	November 22 to December 22	Adventurous, fun-loving, enthusiastic
Capricorn	♑	December 22 to January 21	Serious, hardworking, responsible
Aquarius	♒	January 21 to February 19	Idealistic, humani-tarian, persistent
Pisces	♓	February 19 to March 21	Spiritual, compassion-ate, dreamy

Are you an energetic, take-charge Aries ♈ always starting up new moneymaking schemes, or a balanced Libra ♎ more concerned with creating harmony and investigating principles? These two signs actually do have some common ground. Both Aries and Libra are known as Cardinal signs. Each Cardinal sign signals the beginning of a season, and individuals born at these times are seen to be independent. They like to start projects and move ahead, but can sometimes be impatient. People born under Fixed signs—in the middle of a season—are characterized as determined, reliable, and consistent, but, on the down side, they can be stubborn. Mutable signs come at the end of a season. People born at these times are said to be resourceful and flexible, and they tend to be quick learners. They can, however, lack perseverance. Find your Sun ☉ sign on the following chart, and then think about how your Cardinal, Fixed, or Mutable tendencies are impacting your finances. You may want to spend some time writing about this topic in your notebook.

Astro Sun ☉ Signs and Their Qualities

Cardinal	Fixed	Mutable
Aries ♈	Taurus ♉	Gemini ♊
Cancer ♋	Leo ♌	Virgo ♍
Libra ♎	Scorpio ♏	Sagittarius ♐
Capricorn ♑	Aquarius ♒	Pisces ♓

Number-Two Man

Now we are going to take a closer look at the second-richest man in the world. We are reprinting Warren Buffett's birth chart here so you can get a good view of his astrological balance sheet. Take your own birth chart out, too, and have it handy as your read through these next sections because you will be referring to it often.

First, on the following chart, find Warren's Sun ☉. Notice that there is a number next to the Sun symbol and below that you find the symbol for Virgo ♍. This indicates that at the time of Warren's birth the Sun was in Virgo and that Warren is a Virgo. The numbers next to the Zodiac sign indicate the more precise position of the given planet, in this case the Sun, in the constellation. (Okay, the Sun is not really a planet, but in Astrology it, along with the Moon ☽, is considered to be.) Now, find the Sun ☉ on your own chart.

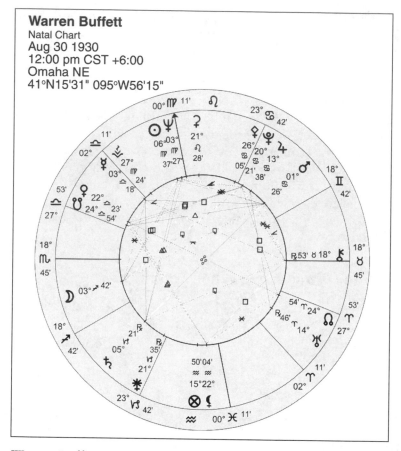

Warren Buffett's astrological birth chart.

Next, notice that the circle that makes up the chart is divided into 12 sections, almost like pie pieces. Each section is called a house. The astrological houses represent different areas of your life.

The horizontal line that divides the chart in two actually does represent the horizon. The heavenly bodies above the line on Warren's chart could have been visible in the sky at the time and place of his birth. On the left end of that line, find the symbol for Scorpio ♏. This placement indicates that the constellation of Scorpio was on the eastern horizon at the time of Warren's birth and was thus rising. So Scorpio is Warren's rising sign. An individual familiar with Astro-speak would say of Warren, "He's a Virgo with Scorpio rising." The rising sign is also called the ascendant. Take a look at your own birth chart and find your ascendant.

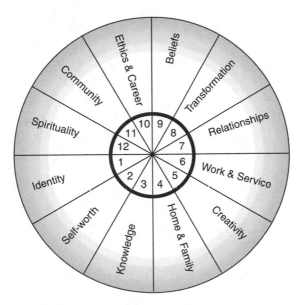

Each of your birth chart's 12 houses represents an area of your life.

Your rising sign, or ascendant, describes the face that you show to the world and the way that you express yourself. So inside you may be a resourceful and practical Virgo ♍ (like Warren), but the face that the world sees is one of passionate and powerful Scorpio ♏. Take a look at the previous list of Zodiac signs and keywords, and make a note of the description of the mask that you wear and show to the world.

The Planets and Their Addresses

Besides your Sun ☉ sign and your ascendant, you have many others signs in your birth chart. In fact, every sign of the Zodiac is represented in this map of the heavens from the time of your birth. Each planet also rests in a sign, which astrologers use kind of like street addresses. But before we start talking about the planets and what sign each one of them is in, let's have you meet the major planets of Astrology.

Planet	Symbol	Keywords
Sun	☉	The self
Moon	☽	Emotions
Mercury	☿	Communication, travel

Planet	Symbol	Keywords
Venus	♀	Love, beauty, personal resources
Mars	♂	Aggression, physical energy
Jupiter	♃	Confidence, vitality, optimism, success
Saturn	♄	Control, limitation
Uranus	♅	Invention, independence, originality, change
Neptune	♆	Creativity, dreams, illusions
Pluto	♇	Power, evolution, destruction, regeneration

As we noted before, the Sun ☉ and Moon ☽ are considered by Astrology to be planets. Because their light is so bright, together they are known as the luminaries. Pay special attention here to the symbol for each planet. You are going to be seeing a lot of these symbols throughout this book. Soon they will look just as familiar to you as $$s and ¢s. Just like the signs, the planets also have their own energies. We've provided keywords for you here to help you get to know them better.

Now, are you ready for some astrological tabulation and some fun? In the following table, fill in the information for each of Warren's planets. We started you off by putting in the information for Warren's Sun ☉. So the first thing you are going to do is find Warren's Moon ☽ on his birth chart. Then, still looking at his birth chart, make a note of which signit is in. Refer to the table of signs earlier in this chapter and record the name of Warren's Moon ☽ sign and the keyword associated with that sign. Then check back and see which house the Moon is in by comparing Warren's chart to the table showing the number and keywords for each house. Once you are done with this exercise, you will have learned the basics of reading an astrological chart and you will have gotten to know Warren Buffett better. And perhaps after spending this time with a multi-billionaire, some of his financial savvy will rub off on you!

Warren Buffett's Planets in Their Signs and Houses

Planet	Planet Keyword	Astro Sign and Symbol	Astro Sign Keyword	House	House Keyword
Sun ☉	Explores	Virgo ♍	Resourceful	10th house	Reputation, career
Moon ☽	_____	_____	_____	_____	_____
Mercury ☿	_____	_____	_____	_____	_____

16

Planet	Planet Keyword	Astro Sign and Symbol	Astro Sign Keyword	House	House Keyword
Venus ♀	_____	_____	_____	_____	_____
Mars ♂	_____	_____	_____	_____	_____
Jupiter ♃	_____	_____	_____	_____	_____
Saturn ♄	_____	_____	_____	_____	_____
Uranus ♅	_____	_____	_____	_____	_____
Neptune ♆	_____	_____	_____	_____	_____
Pluto ♇	_____	_____	_____	_____	_____

Astrological Cycles, Financial Trends

As you have started to see, Astrology can describe you and your personality. It can also speak to larger issues and events around you. Certain astrological cycles, such as eclipses, can have an effect on everyone down here and on their finances. A total eclipse of the Sun ☉ is an extremely dramatic celestial event, and it can signal drama here on Earth, too. (Remember the saying, "As above, so below.") There are other types of eclipses, too, a number of which you won't see in the sky. But even if you can't see them, you'll probably feel the effect of one planet interfering with the energy of another. Both solar and lunar eclipses can shake you up. And they can shake up the stock market and consumer confidence, too.

Eclipses, like the Tower card from the Tarot, can feel like an unexpected jolt. Upright, the Tower indicates a sudden shift or change; reversed, the Tower R may be saying that you are avoiding an issue or a change you need to make.

We discuss other cycles, such as planetary retrogrades, in later chapters. For now, just know that the word "retrograde" ℞ is the astrological term used for the time when a planet appears to be moving backward in the sky from our perspective here on Earth. You may have noticed the retrograde symbol ℞ on Warren Buffett's natal chart; we will talk more about Buffett, his wealth, and those backward-moving planets in Chapter 7.

What Is Money?

If you add up all the time you devote to thinking about money, spending it, and worrying about it, your balance sheet of hours probably adds up to a pretty staggering number. But do you ever really think about money other than as something you want to get and spend? Before you can explore what money means to you, let's think about a more basic question. What is money really?

Our English word *money* comes from a Latin word meaning "money" or "mint," which was derived from *Moneta*, a name for the goddess Juno. Juno was associated with money because her temple in Rome was also the site of the mint where currency was made. We are interested in the fact that Juno, the queen of the gods, who is represented in Astrology by an asteroid that bears her name, is so closely connected to money. Certainly, this connection can serve as evidence that the financial and the spiritual do in fact go together. Furthermore, you could argue that money *is* a matter of spirit. And what better way to investigate a matter of spirit than through the Intuitive Arts? But let's continue this exploration of the word *money*.

Money can be a spiritual issue.

The *American Heritage Dictionary* defines money as "A commodity such as gold or silver that is legally established as an exchangeable equivalent of all other commodities and is used as a measure of their comparative values on the market." The words that jump out at us here are "exchangeable equivalent" and "comparative values." Money is something that you trade or exchange for other things. It represents potential—goods that you could acquire, trips you could take, classes in which you could enroll. As such, money has no inherent value. Its value is determined by what it can bring you.

As you know, the price or comparative value for very similar goods can vary widely. You can buy a pair of shoes for $30 or you can spend $300. Sure, the expensive designer shoes probably have special features and have more prestige attached to them, but both pairs of shoes do the job of protecting your feet. The monetary value of goods is determined by the market. If no one would spend $300 on a pair of shoes, then the value of the shoes would drop and so would the price. Some would argue that comparative values in our society have become skewed. As evidence they point to the fact that people in certain jobs, such as teaching, are underpaid. The value of the services teachers provide is considered to be far greater than the amount of their actual compensation.

Then you also want to consider what value things have for you in more personal terms. If you don't much like coffee, you probably would not want to go to an upscale coffee chain and spend $3 on a tall vanilla latte. Three dollars, or more, for a cup of coffee would seem absurd to you, especially when you can buy a cup for $.75 at the convenience store next door. If, on the other hand, you really love coffee and you really love tall vanilla lattes, $3 may seem a reasonable price to pay. That cup of coffee may mean more to Katherine than it does to Arlene, but they both are still charged the same price. But what are you really paying for? Well, the coffee for starters, but the actual coffee probably only comprises a small percentage of your final price. You also pay for the labor of the employees who make the coffee. And you pay for all the choices that they give you—a whole menu of various kinds of coffees, the different milks to add to the coffee, the machine used to steam the milk for the coffee, the flavored syrups available, and the packages of sugar, just for starters. All those choices can make you feel as if you have really accomplished something and taken a step toward getting what you want.

An important step in achieving your own abundance is to decide what things are worth to you—regardless of their actual price tag.

A trip across the country may be worth more to you than that expensive designer dress or suit, even if the dress or suit has a higher number on its price tag. The real value of the trip versus the clothes all depends on you and on your values. So the real question becomes what has value to you? You may want to spend some time writing about this topic in your notebook.

It may help to think of money as a form of energy. The actual currency—the physical objects that we use, like the dollar bill—represent units of energy. We like the fact that the word *currency* comes from a Latin word that means "a flowing." This word and the word *current,* which we usually think of in terms of electricity, both come from the same Latin word. So you see money does have an energetic connection. And so do the planets in your astrological birth chart, the images on the Tarot cards, and the flashes of insight that you receive from your Psychic Intuition.

Your Money and Your Abundance

Now you are ready to use the Intuitive Arts to help you create your own personal form of abundance. Astrology, Tarot, and your Psychic Intuition will help you determine what it is that you really want and start you on the path to reaching your goals. So with astrological birth chart in hand, your Tarot deck, your Psychic Intuition, and your Intuitive Arts notebook, travel with us and let us show you how to find the abundance you desire. You may learn, like Dorothy in *The Wizard of Oz,* that what you seek, your heart's desire, is in your own backyard, in which case the Intuitive Arts will help you appreciate what you already have. Or you may find that the Intuitive Arts and your newfound insights into yourself and the workings of the financial world prompt you to grow, evolve, and change into a richer and more satisfying relationship to money and your own abundance.

chapter 2

How Much $$ Is Enough?

The haves and the have nots
Yin and *yang* keywords
Yin, yang, and Astrology's financial planets
Yin and *yang* meet Psychic Intuition through Tarot's
Empress and Emperor
Tarot's Seven-Card *yin/yang* Financial Forecast

Do you think about money in black and red terms? You have it (you're in the black) or you don't (you're in the red); you are rich, or you are poor. At some time in our lives, nearly everyone has considered the question: How much $$ would you need to feel … (fill in the blank): safe, loved, happy, rich? How much $$ is enough? The topic of money certainly can cause us to think (and act!) in extreme ways. Yin and yang, the ancient Chinese symbol that represents the balance and unity of opposites, is important to the Intuitive Arts, and it communicates a lot about our perceptions of money. The yin/yang circle contains dark and light, negative and positive, internal and external, surplus and deficit, giving and receiving. Each half of the symbol's balance holds within it the seed of its other half. Does all this make you think about getting and spending? We use Astrology to see how your birth chart reveals your personal yin/yang balance sheet. Psychic Intuition reveals whether you feel like Tarot's Empress or Emperor when it comes to money. You learn what yin and yang really mean in the realm of money and how finding your own personal balance can help you create and maintain abundance in your financial life— and beyond!

Too Little, Too Much

"That Donald Trump, he may be a financial high roller—he's up and he's down, but he'll always come out sitting on top of a pile of money too big to fit in his casino vault in Atlantic City!" Have you ever caught yourself saying something like this? Or thinking, "Oprah, she has more money than God—I wish she'd give *me* some of it. But at least she uses her money well." The perception that someone else has too much money is often accompanied by the sense that you yourself have too little. But is this really true? Certainly comparing yourself to Donald Trump or Oprah Winfrey could make anyone feel he or she were lacking in financial savvy and acumen.

The feeling of lack, of not having enough, drives many people. They work hard, and many of them spend hard. And despite all that they have, they are still certain that they don't have enough, that they must earn *more* and buy *more*. That they must obtain a certain special object—be it a car or a piece of jewelry or a house in the country—that will signify that they have finally made it. Some of these people may never feel satisfied with their lives. They will forever strive to acquire and perpetually fall short of abundance (no matter how large the balance reads on their bank statements and brokerage reports—or on their credit card bills ...) because they are living unbalanced lives.

To feel your own abundance and be able to truly enjoy the fruits of your labors, you need to reach a satisfying balance between your spiritual, emotional, and physical selves. This is a truth that reaches far beyond money. You can have a dollar in your pocket and be the most abundant person in the universe—as free as Tarot's Fool. *Yes!* It's true. Will his walk through life take him on great adventures or send him over the cliff? It doesn't seem that dollar is the determining factor in the Fool's future! Take a look at Tarot's Devil card to see how easy it is to fall prey to materialism and obsession of ownership. Consider the Lovers you see in chains not as a literal representation of a woman and a man, but as the *yin/yang* push and pull of attraction to money and possession that exists within you.

Turn the Fool's pockets inside out and there may not be more than a dollar in that pocket—and he doesn't seem to care! Has Tarot's Devil got you chained to your money and possessions—as well as your fears and strong emotions about how much, or how little, you have?

Determining how much money you actually need is an important step in achieving personal financial balance, and freeing yourself from the Devil's chains. The amount of money you need is not just a simple equation of how much you earn minus how much you spend. You also need to look at the spiritual and emotional issues connected to your cash. You need to look at what you want and ask yourself if money will truly help you obtain those things. If you make investments—whether in the stock market, real estate, artwork, or your own creative output—you need to know how comfortable you are with risk.

You also want to consider your own levels of fear—does the idea of having money, and possibly being able to do more of what you want, scare you? Or does the idea of not having money, of not having "enough" frighten you? Are you a natural risk taker? Or are you risk-averse? In which areas do you have a tendency toward active and out-going behavior? And in which are you more quiet and receptive? Can you work to balance these two energies in the financial realm?

Yin and yang *represent the energies that inform the essential nature of balance and wholeness between extremes.*

Exploring your own personal financial balance sheet through the lens of the ancient Chinese concept of *yin* and *yang* can show you your growth potential and help you achieve equilibrium. Study the image of the *yin/yang* symbol. Note how the black or shadow area, which represents *yin,* and the white or light area, which represents *yang,* intertwine. Notice, too, that the *yin* half contains a spot of *yang* and the *yang* half contains a spot of *yin.* Perhaps employing more of your *yang* or active energies in the financial realm will make you (and your checkbook) more balanced. Maybe you have to get out there and hustle up some business or maybe you need to learn to take more financial risks. On the other hand, you may need to be more *yin* and learn to be still and truly receive what the world has to offer you. Let's explore your financial *yin/yang* equation and start working toward the equilibrium that brings abundance.

Yin and Yang Keywords

In the following table, you'll find some common keywords associated with the *yin/yang* balance. Many people describe these pairings as opposites, but we like to see each half as part of the whole. Remember that within everything that is primarily *yin* lies a bit of *yang.* And within everything primarily *yang* rests some *yin.*

Yin	Yang
Indirect	Direct
Cold	Warm
Receptive	Active

Yin	Yang
Earth	Heaven
Internal	External
Moon	Sun
Feminine	Masculine

Remember, too, that we're talking about energy here. As we observed in the Tarot's Devil card imagery, the feminine/masculine pairing does not necessarily translate literally into female and male—but into the nature of the energy itself. Plenty of women out there are full of *yang* energy! And so, too, can men harbor *yin* energy. Feminine, in this sense, suggests quiet, reflective energy, while masculine indicates a more fiery and active energy. Understanding *yin* and *yang,* the two halves that make up a whole, can help you learn about your approach to (or avoidance of!) personal financial balance.

The Yin and Yang Balance in Astrology

Yin and *yang* appear in Astrology as the energies of the signs of the Zodiac. Half of the 12 signs are ascribed indirect, receptive, or *yin,* energy. The other half of the signs are said to have predominantly direct, active, or *yang,* energy. The following table presents the 12 signs of the Zodiac and their energies.

Yin	Yang
Taurus ♉	Aries ♈
Cancer ♋	Gemini ♊
Virgo ♍	Leo ♌
Scorpio ♏	Libra ♎
Capricorn ♑	Sagittarius ♐
Pisces ♓	Aquarius ♒

Now, knowing that you are a Libra ♎ and that the energy of that sign is direct, active, and *yang* can be useful information. But that doesn't mean that you will have a direct and active approach to your finances. And neither will a Taurus ♉ necessarily be more indirect and receptive in the realm of money. Your astrological birth chart includes all of the signs and their energies within it; the combinations and relationships you find there between these forces create the unique balance that is you.

Looking at your financial planets, you can begin to see a clearer picture of the natural *yin* and *yang* tendencies of your personal balance sheet. Let's look at a few examples—three individuals who've either made their mark on society, reaped huge financial gains, or both—to see how *yin* and *yang* work in the realm of money.

To Risk or Not to Risk

Do you take risks or do you avoid them? Taking appropriate financial risks, whether that means quitting a job that bores you to start your own bed and breakfast, investing in the stock market, or signing on for a position with a start-up company, is an important part of everyone's financial life. Sometimes you have to let go of the sure thing to reach for what you really want. As they say, if you don't play, you can't win. Of course, only you can determine how much risk you and your lifestyle can tolerate. You want to strike a balance between your active risk-taking energies and your more mellow cautious and conservative energies. Sounds like more *yin* and *yang* balance to us!

Following you will find the astrological birth charts for three people who live or have lived in the spotlight. Both Donald Trump and Oprah Winfrey have taken financial risks and gathered great gains. Mohandas Gandhi (1869–1948) came from a prominent family, lived a life of great frugality, and took huge risks as the leader of the Hindu people, the "father of the nation" of India, and a major proponent of nonviolent political action. Take a look at the charts on the following pages and see what you notice about them.

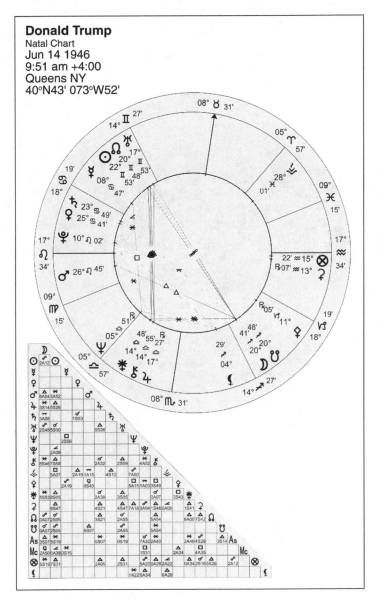

Donald Trump
Natal Chart
Jun 14 1946
9:51 am +4:00
Queens NY
40°N43' 073°W52'

Donald Trump's birth chart.

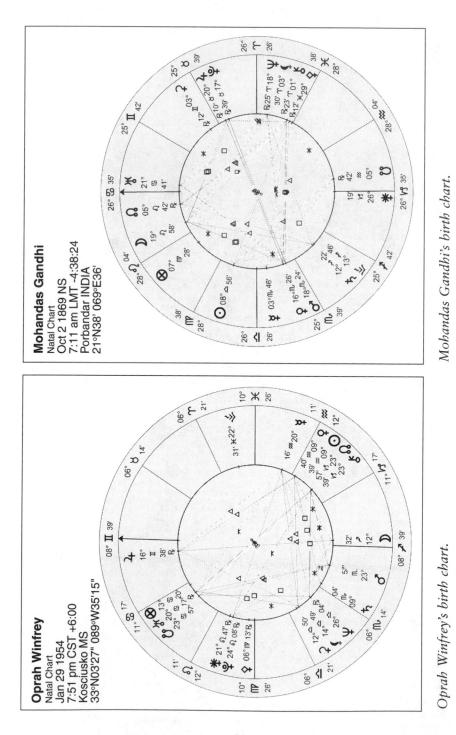

Mohandas Gandhi's birth chart.

Oprah Winfrey's birth chart.

We are going to focus our attention here on the *yin* and *yang* balance of the financial planets—Venus ♀, Mars ♂, Jupiter ♃, and Saturn ♄. If you have some knowledge of Astrology, you will know that Venus and Mars are two of the inner, or personal, planets. The personal planets help to define who you are by manifesting as facets of your personal energy and behavior. Jupiter and Saturn are the two social planets. You will see their energies in the ways that you interact with the world around you.

Venus ♀, of course, is the planet associated with love. Venus also describes your ability to attract money and material well-being. Venus is seen to be generous and giving. The position of Venus in relation to the signs of the Zodiac helps to define the kind of energy you have in relation to money and abundance (and, of course, love, too). For example, Venus in the *yang* signs—Aries ♈, Gemini ♊, Leo ♌, Libra ♎, Sagittarius ♐, and Aquarius ♒—has a more active generosity than Venus in the *yin* signs—Taurus ♉, Cancer ♋, Virgo ♍, Scorpio ♏, Capricorn ♑, and Pisces ♓.

Mars ♂, the planet of action and warrior ways, also describes how you express your aggressive energies and how you act to meet your needs and fulfill your desires. In the financial realm, Mars is also associated with speculation, extreme behavior, and throwing caution to the wind. Mars's energy in your birth chart gets part of its tone from the astrological sign it is in and whether that sign has predominantly *yin* or *yang* energy.

Jupiter ♃ is associated with your vitality, and it represents growth, prosperity, success, and generosity. The energy of Jupiter in the *yang* signs is often described with these words: adventurous, enthusiastic, expansive, generous, innovative, social, zealous. In the *yin* signs, Jupiter's energy is described as hardworking, patient, powerful, pragmatic, serious, steady, and sympathetic.

Saturn's ♄ energy is one of rules and responsibilities. Saturn can be conservative or tightfisted with money. Some astrologers see Saturn as the great teacher, one who will impart to you your life lessons. But others disagree with this view and describe Saturn as malefic and as the symbolic representation of loss.

Now let's look at the balance of energy in Donald Trump's financial planets. You will see in the following table that Trump has two financial planets in *yin* signs and two in *yang* signs. The *yin* and *yang* energies are also balanced between the inner, personal planets Venus ♀ and Mars ♂ and the social planets Jupiter ♃ and Saturn ♄. This balance between *yin* and *yang* would suggest Trump has a steady-enough equilibrium to be able to take appropriate financial risks. His *yang* Mars and Jupiter energies, which can be exuberant, passionate, and lacking in caution, are counterbalanced by his *yin* Venus and Saturn, both of which crave security.

Donald Trump's Astrological Balance Sheet

Financial Planets	Astro Sign	Energy
Venus ♀	Cancer ♋	*Yin*
Mars ♂	Leo ♌	*Yang*
Jupiter ♃	Libra ♎	*Yang*
Saturn ♄	Cancer ♋	*Yin*

Like Trump, Oprah Winfrey has a balance of *yin* and *yang* energies in her financial planets. She also has a *yin/yang* balance between her inner, personal planets and her social planets. Oprah, too, has been able to take appropriate financial risks. Her *yang* Venus ♀ and Jupiter ♃ are offset by the *yin* energies of her Mars ♂ and Saturn ♄. It's interesting to note that Oprah's Venus, a planet associated with generosity and giving, is in a *yang* sign. This placement would indicate that her generous Venus energy is active and outgoing. Oprah's philanthropic contributions, socially conscious work, and the creation of her Angel Network bear out this interpretation of her natural astrological energies.

Oprah Winfrey's Astrological Balance Sheet

Financial Planets	Astro Sign	Energy
Venus ♀	Aquarius ♒	*Yang*
Mars ♂	Scorpio ♏	*Yin*
Jupiter ♃	Gemini ♊	*Yang*
Saturn ♄	Scorpio ♏	*Yin*

Looking at the signs of Mohandas Gandhi's financial planets, you will see an imbalance between *yin* and *yang* energies. Gandhi's personal planets are both in signs with *yin* energy. He has one social planet in a *yin* sign and one in a *yang* sign. This kind of imbalance could indicate a lack of concern about or interest in money or financial difficulties, especially early in life. "Men say I am a saint losing himself in politics," Gandhi once said, describing himself. "The fact is that I am a politician trying my hardest to become a saint." These certainly don't sound like the words of a man who was concerned about his own material well-being.

Gandhi often sacrificed his personal comfort for the good of his cause. Gandhi's *yin* Scorpio ♏ energy can be seen in an extraordinary self-discipline, his willingness to take on long-term hunger strikes, for example. The balanced combination of Gandhi's *yin* Jupiter ♃ and *yang* Saturn ♄ would indicate a steadiness and ability to persevere that is born out by his tireless work on behalf of his nation's independence.

Mohandas Gandhi's Astrological Balance Sheet

Financial Planets	Astro Sign	Energy
Venus ♀	Scorpio ♏	*Yin*
Mars ♂	Scorpio ♏	*Yin*
Jupiter ♃	Taurus ♉	*Yin*
Saturn ♄	Sagittarius ♐	*Yang*

Of course, there is more in Gandhi's birth chart and in Oprah's and Trump's, too, than just Venus ♀, Mars ♂, Jupiter ♃, and Saturn ♄. All of the planets, and the interrelations between them, inform the energy that makes these extraordinary people who they are. And these astrological energies help to inform who you are, too.

Your Astrological Yin and Yang Balance Sheet

To explore your own astrological *yin/yang* balance sheet, you need to look in your birth chart. Locate your Venus ♀, Mars ♂, Jupiter ♃, and Saturn ♄. Use the form below, photocopy it, or draw it in your notebook, and fill in the astrological sign for each planet. Then write in whether the sign in which the planet sits represents predominantly *yin* or *yang* energy.

Financial Planets	Astro Sign	Yin or Yang Energy
Venus ♀	_____	_____
Mars ♂	_____	_____
Jupiter ♃	_____	_____
Saturn ♄	_____	_____

Here are two lists—the symbols for each of the signs and the symbols for the planets. Why not memorize a few of them each day? What? You know them all already? How very *yang* and active of you! Or, have you been being *yin* and receptive through learning?

Astro Sign	Astro Symbol	Planet	Astro Symbol
Aries	♈	Sun	☉
Taurus	♉	Moon	☽
Gemini	♊	Mercury	☿
Cancer	♋	Venus	♀
Leo	♌	Mars	♂
Virgo	♍	Jupiter	♃
Libra	♎	Saturn	♄
Scorpio	♏	Uranus	♅
Sagittarius	♐	Neptune	♆
Capricorn	♑	Pluto	♇
Aquarius	♒		
Pisces	♓		

After you've noted the sign for each of your financial planets in your table, use the following chart to determine which of those signs represent *yin* energy and which represent *yang* energy. Then record your results on your personal financial planets table.

Yin	Yang
Taurus ♉	Aries ♈
Cancer ♋	Gemini ♊
Virgo ♍	Leo ♌
Scorpio ♏	Libra ♎
Capricorn ♑	Sagittarius ♐
Pisces ♓	Aquarius ♒

How is your energy balanced among your financial planets? (Arlene's is balanced, but Katherine's tips toward the *yin*.) Keep in mind that if you have found an imbalance, that does not mean that you are incapable of taking financial risks or that you will only take bad ones. The energies of your financial planets only describe your natural tendencies. Some of us are natural risk takers, and some of us need a little prodding!

Remember, despite any *yin/yang* tendencies you may have, you still have *free will*. You can exercise your free will and learn to take appropriate financial risks, make investments, earn, spend, and enjoy what life has to offer. And keep in mind, too, that Astrology is just one way of looking at your personal *yin/yang* balance sheet. We talk more about your natural tendencies toward either *yin* or *yang* energy, and look at ways you can tip your own scales toward balance.

Yin and Yang Revealed Through Psychic Intuition

In your financial life, do you tend to be more direct and active (*yang*) or indirect and receptive (*yin*)? In American society, we place a lot of emphasis on the active. We say that it is better to give than to receive. We are always running and doing, earning and scheming as to how to earn more. Striking a balance between active *yang* energies and receptive *yin* energies, between working to obtain and receiving, can help you to achieve your own sense of abundance.

You could run to the library and begin a research project on personal finance and abundance. Or you could take a more *yin* approach, get quiet, and use your Psychic Intuition to explore your own inner financial balance and what you need to do to give yourself a better sense of equilibrium. Here's an exercise to help you do just that.

Queen (and King) for a Day

We're going to use the Tarot cards as a jumping-off point for your Psychic Intuition; so, okay Fool, get ready to jump off that cliff into the unknown of your deepest self! Find some time when you can be alone and quiet (and *yin*). Find the Empress and the Emperor cards in your Tarot deck. Clear off a spot on a table and place the cards side by side with the Empress on the left and the Emperor on the right. (If you don't have a set of cards, you can use the illustrations in this book.) Make sure that you have your Intuitive Arts notebook and a pen that you like nearby.

A nice pair from the Major Arcana—the Empress and the Emperor.

They look like a pretty balanced and complementary couple, don't you think? Start by examining the Empress. Study the wheat at her feet, the trees in the background, the flowing water that runs toward her. Note her clothing, jewelry, and comfortable padded seat.

Close your eyes and see if you can conjure up her image in your mind's eye. Open your eyes again and gaze at her card. Concentrate on the details that you missed. Try this a few times. Once you feel that you can "see" her pretty accurately in your mind's eye, keep your eyes closed.

Now imagine that you are her (and, remember, her energy is metaphorical). Feel the clothes against your skin, the necklace resting against your collarbones, the star-bedecked crown on your head. Allow yourself to sink into the comfort of the cushions that support you. Grasp your scepter, and feel its weight. Soak in the glory of the golden sky. Hear the sounds of the stream burbling toward you. What else do you hear? Smell the wheat that surrounds you, the gentle breeze wafting from the trees. What else do you smell? Is there a taste of something sweet and delicious in your mouth?

Spend some time on each of your senses until you can really inhabit her. Feel the easy, sensuous delight that it is to be the Empress. You are surrounded by abundance, and you are receptive to that abundance. When you feel permeated with Empress energy, open your eyes.

In your notebook, write about what it felt like to be the Empress. Hold on to the feeling of her, and make a list of 10 things that you have and love. Close your eyes and picture the things on this list. Allow yourself to receive these gifts.

Now make a list of 10 things that you want. Remember the Empress and imagine yourself receiving the items on this list. Imagining these things with as many sensory details as possible will help to lead you down the path to both obtaining and enjoying them. Make some notes in your notebook if you feel the need, or draw a picture before you move on to this exercise's next step.

Turn your attention to the Emperor. Study his throne, the mountains behind him, and his well-armored boots. Examine his scepter, which ends in an Egyptian ankh, a symbol of wisdom. In the same way that you did with the Empress, work toward being able to conjure up his image in your mind's eye. Once you can "see" the Emperor with your eyes closed, imagine that you are him (once again, his energy is metaphorical).

Feel the cape around your shoulders, the crown on your head, and the powerful boots protecting your legs and feet. Straighten your spine against the authority of your throne, and feel the strength of your leg muscles. Clasp your scepter, the symbol of your wisdom. Enjoy the weight of the globe in your other hand. Soak in the power of the mountains behind you. Hear the sounds of the stream that flows between you and the mountains. What else do you hear? What do you smell? And what do you taste?

Spend some time on each of your senses until you can really inhabit the Emperor. Feel the assurance and sense of power that it is to be the Emperor. You are wise and hold the world in your hand. You can achieve anything you want to achieve. When you feel permeated with Emperor energy, open your eyes.

In your notebook, write about what it felt like to be the Emperor. Hold on to the feeling of him, and take out your list of 10 things that you have and love from the earlier part of this exercise. Close your eyes and picture the things on this list. Remember the actions you took to obtain these things that you love.

Now look at your list of 10 things that you want. Remember the Emperor and imagine yourself acting to obtain the items on this list. Image your activities toward these goals with as many sensory details as possible. Soon you may find yourself striding down the path to both obtaining and enjoying these things.

From doing this exercise, you should be able to feel how *yin*, in the form of the Empress, and *yang*, in the form of the Emperor, work together. Whenever you feel yourself out of balance, check in, remember what it felt like to be the Empress, and then remember what it felt like to be the Emperor. These feelings can help you reestablish your *yin/yang* equilibrium between being active and receptive that yields satisfaction and true abundance.

Yin and Yang and the Tarot

The Minor Arcana suit associated with possessions, wealth, and security is Pentacles. These are the cards that speak to you about the material world—money, investments, possessions, and your home. Naturally Pentacle cards are also associated with the Element of Earth (we talk more about the Elements in the next chapter), and Earth is associated with *yin* or receptive energy. We think it is no coincidence that money, the quantity we all spend so much *yang* energy actively pursuing, is associated with *yin* forces. Could the cards themselves be telling us as a culture that we need to learn to be more *yin*, to receive and enjoy (and even *notice!*) the wealth that is all around us?

Tarot's Ace of Pentacles shows the yang *energy needed to grow your finances, while also depicting the* yin *earthy garden that balances and blossoms all active pursuits.*

While the Major Arcana cards of the Tarot don't have assigned *yin/yang* labels, you can see this dual but united energy reflected in the cards' imagery. Let's use the Empress and the Emperor as examples. You could easily say that the Empress represents *yin* energy, and the Emperor embodies *yang* energy. We just did! The serenity and sense of ease and comfort presented by the Empress certainly feels like *yin* energy. The fiery colors and somewhat wary expression of the Emperor would tend to support the view of this card's energy as *yang*. Psychiatrist Carl Jung has described the Empress as the Anima, or the feminine side of the self, and the Emperor as the Animus, or masculine side of the self. (Everyone, male or female, has both an Anima and an Animus.) If you did the exercise earlier in this chapter, did you feel the receptive Empress part of yourself opening up? And what about your inner Emperor? Did you feel his active *yang* energy ready to pounce on the next opportunity?

You could also dig a little further into the images and associations of each card. The Empress is associated with Venus ♀, a planet traditionally associated with feminine, receptive, and *yin* energies. But note that Venus rules both Taurus ♉, a *yin* sign, and Libra ♎, a *yang* sign. So what might appear on the surface to be a pure representation of *yin* energy also contains some *yang*, just as the dark area of the *yin/yang* diagram earlier in this chapter contains some light.

The Emperor is associated with Mars ♂, a planet associated with masculine, active, and *yang* energies. Mars rules the sign of Aries ♈, a *yang* sign, and in addition co-rules Scorpio ♏, a *yin* sign. Once again both energies are present. The Emperor's representation of *yang* energy contains a little *yin*, just as the light area of the *yin/yang* diagram contains a little dot of darkness.

The Empress and the Emperor might not come up in every Tarot reading having to do with money. And you might not see many Pentacles either, but with or without them, the cards can be powerful tools to help you define and refine what you want and plan the ways you will work to obtain and receive these things.

A Sample Tarot Spread: Time for a Financial Risk?

Before you ask the Tarot cards if this is the right time for you to use some of your *yang* energy and take steps toward a financial risk, we're going to show you a Seven-Card Financial Forecast Spread that answers just that type of question. A Seven-Card Spread is useful when you are seeking an answer to a yes or no question, but also want a little more depth and wisdom. This spread used to be called the Magic Seven Spread. And these spreads can feel magical! The number 7 is the number of higher knowledge, introspection, and wisdom, after all. It is also the number of Tarot's Major Arcana card, the Chariot. In the Chariot's imagery, we see the representation of opposing forces with the charioteer attempting to balance and center them. But he holds no reins! The balance of the charioteer is achieved through his own inner balance of *yin* and *yang* energies that steadies him in a universe of opposites.

In a Seven-Card Spread, you lay the cards out in a row, starting on the left and moving right. The first two cards of your spread represent the past. Cards three, four, and five describe your present condition, and the last two cards represent your future prospects and potential.

The week of his reading, Gary wanted to know if he should take a financial risk that could possibly bring him great gains. Gary asked his question: *"Should I buy stock this week in the corporations I have been thinking about?"*

The charioteer finds his yin/yang balance.

Arlene had Gary shuffle the cards until she felt they were ready. She had him cut the deck. Then Arlene dealt out a Seven-Card Spread, starting on the left and moving right, to answer Gary's question. Here is his Seven-Card Spread:

Gary's Seven-Card Spread: "Should I buy stock this week in the corporations I have been thinking about?"

The Past: We can see from the 3 of Wands that Gary has had some success in the financial world through strong partnerships and the co-operation of others. He has, though, had some difficulty, 2 of Swords, in the recent past making decisions about his financial dealings.

The Present: The 5 of Pentacles represents Gary's feeling that he, like the people on the card, has been left out in the cold. He feels impoverished. And yet he has a good *yin/yang* balance, 2 of Pentacles, in his present situation and is able to juggle his funds, despite his difficulties. Gary is able to maintain his equilibrium even though he is not financially happy because he has surrendered to his higher wisdom, the Hanged Man. He accepts what is and is open to possibility.

The Future: While the Ace of Pentacles does represent the beginning of prosperity, it also suggests that Gary will make slow headway toward his financial goals. The 2 of Cups R, on the other hand, indicates loss of balance or misunderstanding. Has Gary perhaps misinterpreted data from some of the companies he has his eye on?

Arlene summed up Gary's reading by saying, "Wait, wait, wait!" And despite Gary's feelings of lack, he is in a good position to wait and abide with his *yin* energies. While he is waiting, we think Gary may learn something about himself—what his true needs are and how much money is actually enough for him. Who knows? What he learns may allow him to see his financial needs in a new light and that insight, in turn, may open up a whole new avenue of opportunity.

Your Own Seven-Card Financial Forecast

Now that you've studied Gary's Seven-Card Financial Forecast Spread, you can try one of your own. Word your question so that it is specific. Notice that Gary had particular companies in mind. He did not ask if he should buy stock in general. Gary's question also specified a time frame. He asked if he should buy stock "this week" and not at some undetermined time in the future.

When thinking about your question and how to phrase it, you will probably want to keep in mind your *yin/yang* balance. You could focus on financial risks. You could ask a question about whether you should use your *yang* energies to be active in the financial realm. Or you could ask a question that homes in on your own receptive and *yin* energies. Whatever you ask, make sure it is a question that you really want answered, because the cards will give you an answer.

Write your question here:

_____

Contemplate your question as you shuffle the cards in your Tarot deck. Shuffle until you feel the cards are ready to give you an answer. When you are done shuffling, cut the cards and lay out the seven cards, starting on the left and moving right. Deal the cards with the intent and focus of Tarot's charioteer. Remember: *The first two cards represent your past, the next three cards are your present, and the last two cards represent your future.*

Study the Tarot cards in the spread you have dealt. Try not to look at the Tarot card money keyword meanings we've provided in Appendix B right away. See what the cards say to you first. You may want to look at the cards in the spread as describing a story about you and your question. Notice how the cards' imagery makes you feel. You may be struck by an image in your spread that clearly connects to your question. In Gary's spread, for example, the impoverished people out in the snow in the 5 of Pentacles and the upside-down partners in the 2 of Cups R seemed to indicate caution as the order of the day.

Use the following form to record the cards in your Seven-Card Spread. Jot down your initial thoughts and feelings about these cards, as well. When you are done, go ahead and take a look at Appendix B and the financial card interpretations we have provided. But do so only if you feel you need more information or if your intuitive reading of the cards does not make sense to you. Trust your gut and its innate sense of balance.

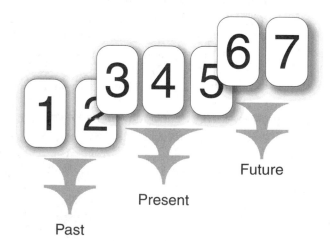

Tarot's Seven-Card Financial Forecast Spread.

We hope you find the answer you are hoping for! Either way, though, your exploration of your own *yin* and *yang* energies in the financial realm will help you make decisions and plan for your future. Recognizing the intertwining nature of *yin* and *yang* energies will help you to go after the money and the true abundance you want. This new awareness will also allow you to enjoy what you already have. We hope that you have come to value and respect both your active *yang* side and your receptive *yin* side. Remember the Empress and the Emperor and how royal it felt to have that kind of balance.

You have contemplated some of the issues involved in taking a financial risk, and you have explored what your own natural tendencies are in this area. We hope that our discussion of *yin* and *yang* has helped you to see your own abundance situation for what it really is. Maybe you still think that Donald Trump has too much money, or wish that Oprah would share a little bit with *you,* but we hope that you have been able to feel and appreciate all of your *own* assets—your quiet, receptive *yin* self and your dynamic, active *yang* self, both of which contain the seeds of each other and when planted, blossom with abundance.

chapter 3

True Abundance Is Elemental

The Elements—Fire, Water, Air, and Earth—they surround you. When it comes right down to it, the Elements are the component parts of all the things that you own and all the things that you want. The hot new best-selling book, a pizza, a new hybrid car, a house in the country—they are all made up of the four Elements. The Elements are also energies. We explore how the Elemental imagery of the Tarot paints a picture of your financial intensity. Use Psychic Intuition to draw your asset portfolio at-a-glance. And use Astrology to plot your Elemental Abundance Signature. Harnessing the power of the Elements can help you to determine, envision, and create your own future abundance.

Elementary Elements

Each of the four Elements is both a physical substance and an energy. Along with *yin* and *yang*, the Elements are a simple way of understanding the forces around you and the facets of your personality and the personalities of others. In the realms of Astrology, Tarot, and

Psychic Intuition, we instantly know a number of things about some-one or something when we are able to define the Elemental energy associated with that person or thing.

You can tap into this knowledge, too, and use it to help you under-stand yourself, your goals and desires surrounding money and wealth, and how to take steps toward attaining the abundance you want in life. Go back to the Empress and Emperor in Chapter 2 and look at your lists you created in your notebook of the 10 things you have and love and the 10 things you want the most—as well as the actions you need to take to manifest them. As you read this chapter, tune your Psychic Intuition to see what energy—Fire, Water, Air, or Earth—will help you get what you want. Consider, too, if this is an energy you already use and feel comfortable with, or if it is one that you need to cultivate.

In Astrology, each sign of the Zodiac is associated with an Element. Aries ♈, Leo ♌, and Sagittarius ♐ are Fire signs. Cancer ♋, Scorpio ♏, and Pisces ♓ are Water signs. Gemini ♊, Libra ♎, and Aquarius ♒ are the Air signs, and Taurus ♉, Virgo ♍, and Capricorn ♑ embody Earth energy.

In the Tarot, each suit of the Minor Arcana is associated with an Element. Wands represent Fire, Cups are associated with Water, Swords are associated with Air, and Pentacles represent the Element of Earth. Just as the Major Arcana cards of the Tarot follow a path from the Fool to the World, the suits of the Minor Arcana show a progression.

You begin with Wands. As Arlene likes to explain it, Wands are your enthusiasm, desire, and sense of enterprise. It's what helps you get out of bed in the morning. It's the Fire and passion that you put into your work. Then you move to Cups, which represent emotion, your attachment to what you do, your belief in what you do, and feelings of service to the public. Then you add Swords, which represent how you think about money, your attitude, and the logic that you use. These rational "head" qualities combine with your emotional "heart" quali-ties, so that ideally your thoughts about your work and money are also connected to your heart. Finally you reach Pentacles, the material plane, the end result, the physical reward, your paycheck.

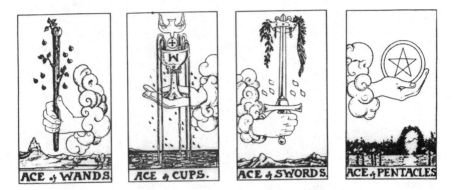

Tarot's Minor Arcana suits initiate an evolution from the Wand of enthusiasm to the Cup of belief, to the Sword's action, to the Pentacle's material result.

Elementary Intuition

Your Psychic Intuition will probably tell you a lot about each Element. Fire energy is passion, enthusiasm, and courage. In your Intuitive Arts notebook, write down some other words that you and your gut associate with the Element of Fire. For Water we would say emotional, intuitive, and flowing. What does your gut tell you about Water and its energy? For Air we came up with mental, thoughtful, and inventive. Do you agree? And for Earth, physical, practical, and hardworking.

What does your intuition tell *you?* In the following table, write words you feel resonate to each Element's energy. Circle the Element you feel most in harmony with in your life. Star the Element that best describes you and your money.

Fire	Water	Air	Earth

Keep this list of your first impressions of the Elements. After you complete the exercises in this chapter, reread what you have written and see if your feelings about the Elements change or stay the same. But right now we are going to delve further into the Elements and their intense power to shape and inform your relationship to money and abundance.

Elemental Intensity

The power of each Element has a number of different manifestations and intents. Just as fire can be embodied in the flame of a match, in a campfire, a burning building, or an out-of-control forest fire, the Element of Fire can manifest itself in your financial life in many forms. To better understand the power of the four Elements, let's use the Tarot cards and take a look at the variable intensity of Fire, Water, Air, and Earth—and how they influence your abundance yield.

Fire in Abundance

The Element of Fire has *yang* energy. Fire represents the passion, desire, and enthusiasm burning inside you. Fire is also associated with courage and transformation. Think of the image of the Phoenix rising from the ashes. The Element of Fire can be the spark of opportunity that helps you to grow, change, and seek new business ventures and moneymaking opportunities. It can be your passion for beauty and your passionate interest in art that drives you into financial action. It can be your enthusiasm for the work that you do. On the flip side, Fire can manifest as a short fuse and a bad temper leading you to burn your bridges and restrict yourself and your opportunities. Fire can also be the money that burns a hole in your pocket—gone before you even knew you had it.

Fire's Energy	Astro Signs	Astro Planets	Tarot Suit
Yang	Aries ♈	Mars ♂ and Pluto ♀	Wands
	Leo ♌	Sun ☉	
	Sagittarius ♐	Jupiter ♃	

Let's look at Tarot's Hermit, the Devil, and the Tower; pull them out of your deck or study the following images. Fire energy can ignite your hopes for your abundance with a steady flame, or you may find yourself quite literally burned until you learn to harness Fire energy for your abundance benefit.

Tarot's Hermit card represents wisdom and wise counsel. As in many of the cards of the Major Arcana, all four Elements appear in the Hermit. Here we focus on the lamp in the Hermit's hand. He carries the Lantern of Truth, which contains a glowing and fiery six-pointed star. The Fire energy depicted here is fairly gentle. It sheds light on the truth and allows the Hermit to see the *real* issues surrounding his situation with pure clarity—no illusions here. (Ralph Kramden of *The Honeymooners* would have a hard time convincing the Hermit to buy those shares in the Brooklyn Bridge!)

Invest in your abundance future by the Hermit's steady glow and you'll avoid getting burned by the Devil, or flaming out in the Tower's conflagration.

If you will let it, your own Fire energy, in the form of your passion, can help you to see the truth, too. The Hermit's light can lead you to acknowledge whether you are on a wise course to abundance, and provide the steady glow to guide you in making a plan to get what you want, and fuel your passion as you act to achieve your goals. Before you begin any financial planning session—whether it be simply paying your bills, doing a budget for a home-improvement project, or laying out a five-year plan—return to Tarot's Hermit and place him on your desk as you are doing the numbers, where he can hold his lantern high to illuminate your plans and calculations.

Tarot's Devil—we've seen him before in this book—represents materialism and obsessions, and as such the card in its wholeness relates to both the Elements of Earth and of Fire. Fire's obsessive intensity is what we experience in the Devil card! Notice the burning torch in the Devil's hand. The Devil appears to be burning the man with the torch's flames, and in fact, the man's tail is on fire. The Lovers literally burn up with passion, but are chained and so cannot act. Remember the man and woman in the Devil card are pictures of your own *yin* and *yang* energies. Fire has got you by the tail, but you don't even seem to know or care when you are under the sway of the Devil.

The Hermit's wise counsel is of no use here! Reversed, the lantern falls from his hands and leaves you in the Devil's dark dungeon, lit only by the flame of your own desire. If you're like us, you probably don't have to spend much effort in meditation to identify the areas of your financial life where the Devil's got you—maybe like Carrie in *Sex and the City* you own 100 pair of shoes at $400 per pair, but don't have money for a down payment on an apartment. Maybe you own 10 bikes—let's see … a road bike, a mountain bike, a tandem … Or you are a perpetual student, investing in class after class but never focusing on one major to obtain the degree that opens doors to your fortune.

There is a flip side to the Devil's fire. Reversed, the Devil represents letting go of obsession or kicking an addiction. The Lovers gain power over the Devil—the man's tail a torch to fend off the monster. The Lovers use the strength of their passionate Fire power, one of the forces that got them into difficulty to begin with, to overcome their problems. If you are chained to an obsession that holds you back from financial freedom, you can learn to harness your passion and allow that force to work *for* you, instead of *against* you. Use the Devil R as an affirming reminder to stay the Hermit's wise course; hang the Devil reversed on your refrigerator door if need be or paste him to that shoebox. Gain confidence that the Devil's fire doesn't have to bite you in your financial, well, you know where!

Tarot's Tower card represents the unexpected, and the unexpected can be good or not so good. The Element of Fire is quite prominent in the Tower. Struck by lightning, it bursts into flames. Fire energy appears here both as lightning and as leaping flames, letting loose its full power. This power seems to manifest in a destructive way, but sometimes you do have to get hit with a lightning bolt to jolt you from your Devil's chains. As you fling yourself from the castle, you can burn your bridges to make a real change and move on with your life.

Use this intense Fire power to burn up a bad financial habit or harness this powerful energy to help you work hard and enable you to incinerate all of your old debts. The Hermit's wise glow grows brighter and clearer thanks to the Tower's jolt of sanity. Reversed, the people in the Tower seem to be cushioned by clouds; their fall is broken by their own new clear vision. Whenever the Tower card comes up in a reading about money, either upright or reversed, be aware that you might experience a jolt in some area of your life before you can manifest a path to well-being and abundance—and this is a *good* thing.

Take a moment to imagine yourself as each of the Fire cards we have just examined. Make a note of which types of Fire are easy and natural for you to try on and which seem more foreign. In your note-book, write a short paragraph for each card about an event, instance, or feeling relating to money and your financial life in which you displayed the kind of energy depicted.

Water in Abundance

The Element of Water has *yin* energy. Water is associated with the emotions, intuition, the subconscious, psychic ability, and cleansing. Water energy can help you go with the flow and follow your intuition to opportunity and abundance. But the flip side of Water can leave you weepy. If you have too much of Water energy in your approach to finances, your money could go Watery and elusive on you and trickle through your fingers. Or you may end up flooded with debt, which at first take might sound expansive—in a flood, Water is certainly expanding, but such a situation can wash away all your benefits and leave you stranded on a dry and deserted island.

Water's Energy	Astro Signs	Astro Planets	Tarot Suit
Yin	Cancer ♋	Moon ☽	Cups
	Scorpio ♏	Mars ♂ and Pluto ♀	
	Pisces ♓	Jupiter ♃ and Neptune ♆	

Look at Tarot's Temperance, the Star, and the Moon; pull them out of your deck or examine the images printed below. Water energy can connect you to the considered flow of your intuitive investment acumen, it can inspire you as you dip your toes into magic depths, or you may find yourself submerged beneath murky impulses you don't understand.

Tarot's Temperance card is all about patience and adaptation. When this card comes up in a reading, it's telling you to slow down, focus your intent, and calmly attend to and manage the flow. Here, the archangel Michael stands on the bank of a body of water with one foot in the water and one foot on land. He has achieved a balance between Water and emotion on the one side and Earth and the material plane on the other. He has tempered his emotions so that he is able to pour water from one chalice to another with a sense of balance and power. How well do you use Temperance's water energy in manifesting your abundance? Are you impatient, spilling water, losing resources, shifting from foot to foot, like the Temperance card in its reversed position? Do you make financial decisions on impulse, without attention? If so, keep the Temperance card in your wallet and let it remind you to make decisions about money in a focused, mindful way that puts you in control and keeps your checkbook in balance!

Manifest your abundance goals with the flowing intent of Tarot's Temperance as you harness the Star's magic waters; be aware, however, of the Moon's pull to the creatures lurking in the murky depths below.

Tarot's Star represents hope and faith. A serene, nude woman pours out water from two urns. Like the archangel Michael, she stands with one foot on land and one in the Water. One of her urns empties onto land, which represents Earth and the material world. She pours the water from the other urn into the pool of water at her feet. The pool represents emotions and imagination. Both in her physical stance and in her pouring action, the woman remains grounded on Earth while she allows herself to explore the inspiring flow of Water's intuition.

Here Water, emotion, and intuition are a serene force, but a force nonetheless. The Element of Water in this card says that if you can harness your intuition in a grounded way, you can see your abundant future, and you have the inspiration to make it so. The next time your partner tells you you're hatching some harebrained scheme—where the stars fall out of the sky as in the Star card reversed, look at the Star upright and meditate on whether you've got that perfect balance between a firm, logical foundation and the intuition that will lead you to the stars!

Tarot's Moon is another Watery card that talks to you about the power of your dreams, imagination, and emotions. This card also speaks of unforeseen events and emotional outbursts. Here a tame dog and a wild wolf (could they be the *yin* and *yang* energies of the canine world?) howl at the Moon, the heavenly body associated with the Element of Water. Once again, the pool of water represents the imagination and emotions and, here, the subconscious. A crayfish crawls out of the water of the subconscious, but is this animal friendly or vicious?

The energy of the Element of Water in the Moon card feels wilder and more unpredictable than the Water energy depicted in Temperance or the Star. The Moon and its Watery energy seem to contain an implicit warning—things are not always what they seem. Your imagination and emotions can, like the dog, be your friend or they can be wild and take an unpleasant turn, if you let them. Is the Moon sending you to emotional extremes about your financial situation, forcing you to think less and less clearly about the issues surrounding you? Reverse the card's energy and turn on the light of the Sun and Moon's *yin/yang* balance that brings the Hermit's illumination and clarity.

Take a moment to imagine yourself as each of the Water cards we have just looked at. Make a note of which energies are easy and natural for you to feel and which seem more foreign. In your notebook, write a short paragraph for each card about an event, instance, or emotional state relating to money and your financial life in which you displayed the kind of energy depicted.

Air in Abundance

The Element of Air has *yang* energy. Air is the province of the intellect, education, computers, wind, and all sounds, including music. Air is the energy you use for all forms of communication. Air is also linked to creativity, meditation, and divination. The energy of Air moves quickly. Air also is the breath of life. The Element of Air can be your ideas about money and your inventiveness. In the phrase "she lives on air," you see someone who needs very little. In this sense, Air is expansive, helping you to attain and giving you what you need. Having your head in the clouds, though, can be restrictive. You might not see a great opportunity down here on the ground. And that lack of grounding could allow you to be blown sideways through your life. Air can also be holes in your pockets that allow your fortune to scatter to the winds.

*The Queen of Swords cuts to the quick, employing the Lovers'
lofty learning to achieve abundance—avoiding the fate of the
Hanged Man caught in a stagnant, motionless atmosphere.*

Air's Energy	Astro Signs	Astro Planets	Tarot Suit
Yang	Gemini ♊	Mercury ☿	Swords
	Libra ♎	Venus ♀	
	Aquarius ♒	Saturn ♄	
		and Uranus ♅	

Let's look at the Queen of Swords, the Lovers, and the Hanged
Man; pull them out of your deck or study the images printed below.
Air energy can cut through to the heart of any financial decision or
situation, can help you use your knowledge to inspire the winds of
change, or can leave you flapping in the breeze.

Tarot's Queen of Swords is a Minor Arcana card worth considering
for the precise Air energy it represents. The Queen of Swords is an
advisor and an astute thinker. The Queen and her sword of razor-like
wit seem to dominate the thick clouds of trouble in the background.
Thus, the Queen has overcome difficulties through the strength of her
logic and intellect. Like the Queen, you can use the power of Air, of
your rational mind, to subdue your own financial clouds and allow
yourself to enjoy clear skies. It takes only your free will to turn this
reversed Queen, sword falling from her hand, upright again.

Tarot's Lovers, freed from the Devil's chains are about inspiration,
choices, and romance, as well as a desire for blissful *yin/yang* harmony.
The word *inspiration* denotes both the excitement that comes from the
stimulation of the mind and senses and the act of inhalation, which is

certainly the province of Air! This card is dominated by the figure of Raphael, the angel of the Air. He is dispensing his inspiration to the man and woman in the foreground—no more Devil. The woman stands in front of the Tree of Knowledge, and the man poses near a tree representing the 12 signs of the Zodiac.

This couple has an abundance of esoteric knowledge and Air power at their disposal, and so do you. You can use this angelically inspired form of Air energy to create harmony in your life, perhaps by using your deep knowledge to research that retirement plan or start that college fund for your kids, determine whether to buy that particular house, or decide how to allocate your investments. Whenever you feel the Lovers R pulling you toward the Devil's chains, remember you only need a fresh breath of Air to return you to equilibrium.

Tarot's Hanged Man card represents surrender to a higher wisdom. In the beneficial application of this card's energies, the man is hanging by a thread, literally suspended in Air, and yet he appears to be in a calm, meditative state. Because he is both mindful and thoughtful (both qualities associated with Air), he has accepted his past and is open to whatever the future will bring. His is a quiet and focused mind that has tapped into the stillness of Air by looking inside. But watch out for situations where you become stagnant and motionless or so caught in contemplation that you forget to act! The Hanged Man in reversed position is ready to make his move and take the Queen's swords into action.

Take a moment to imagine yourself as each of the Air cards we have just looked at. Make a note of which types of Air are easy and natural for you to imagine and which seem more foreign. In your notebook, write a short paragraph for each card about an event, instance, or idea relating to money and your financial life in which you displayed the kind of energy depicted.

Earth in Abundance

The Element of Earth has *yin* energy. Earth represents the material world. The Element of Earth is associated with growth, stability, healing, and abundance. Earth also represents money and prosperity and is associated with practical activities and hard work. Earth energy can help you to feel comfortably rooted, stable, and secure. Too much Earth energy can make it hard for you to resist the pull of gravity, leaving you stuck in the mud. Unable to act positively in such a situation, you may start to behave as if money really does grow on trees.

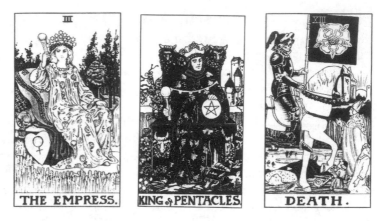

The Empress enjoys her abundant powers as the King of Pentacles measures his yield, while Death champions the advantages of reaping and sowing anew.

Earth's Energy	Astro Signs	Astro Planets	Tarot Suit
Yin	Taurus ♉	Venus ♀	Pentacles
	Virgo ♍	Mercury ☿	
	Capricorn ♑	Saturn ♄	

   Look at Tarot's Empress, King of Pentacles, and Death; pull them out of your deck or study the images printed here. Earth energy can root itself in a foundation of grounded investment and growth that yields abundant harvest overflowing, or it can clear the field for a new cycle of planting and potential income.

   Tarot's Empress represents abundance and fertility through the Earth Mother, comfortably settled on her throne among the bounty of nature. She is open to the pleasure of creature comforts, and she enjoys her physicality. She embodies a loving and sensuous Earth energy. Are you enjoying a fertile period of abundant growth? Carry Tarot's Empress card with you as an invitation to bring rooted, ripe success and comfort to your financial future!

   Tarot's King of Pentacles represents the steadfast, prosperous, and benevolent aspects of Earth energy. His face appears friendly and easy-going, and yet there is something almost uncanny about him. His body blends into his throne as if he were growing out of it. The embroidered grapevines on his robes almost appear to be real. He could just about be half plant and half human. Clearly, this king has the knack to increase any investment or grow any portfolio! But reversed, his steadfast and hardworking energy can turn dark and become stubbornness and a bullheaded materialism. At his best, the King of Pentacles is as gifted as the Oracle of Omaha, Warren Buffett. At his worst, this King more closely resembles the infamous character Mr. Potter in Frank Capra's classic *It's a Wonderful Life.* ("Potter's not selling, he's *buying!*")

Tarot's **Death** card represents, well, death in a metaphorical sense. This card speaks of regeneration, transformation, and rebirth. When this card comes upright in a reading, it indicates a major change; when reversed, it indicates delay and stagnation. As Earth energy, this card shows us the flowing nature of all life. The seasons change, and with them the Earth changes. Plants sprout, grow, bear fruit, and die back. As human beings, we also participate in this life cycle. This type of Earth energy can feel dark, but it is the darkness that nurtures the seeds before they crack open and burst forth with new life.

Take a moment to imagine yourself as each of the Earth cards we have just looked at. Make a note of which energies are easy and natural for you to inhabit and which seem more foreign. In your notebook, write a short paragraph for each card about an event, instance, or emotional state relating to money and your financial life in which you displayed the kind of energy depicted.

Elemental Asset Allocation

Now you are gaining an intuitive sense of the Elemental energies you tend to express in the way you relate to money and abundance. Make a visual representation of the Elemental energies in your financial life. We like to think of this diagram as your own personal Elemental Asset Allocation.

Katherine's personal Elemental Asset Allocation looks like this:

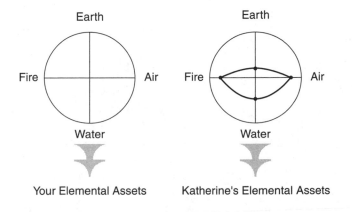

Your Elemental Assets   Katherine's Elemental Assets

You would probably be right if you said that Katherine's head is often in the clouds and her feet don't quite reach the ground! To give herself a better balance, Katherine tries to lay off coffee, drink a lot of water, and practice a very grounding form of yoga. Now, map out your own personal Elemental Asset Allocation. On the cusp for each Element, draw a dot on the line where you feel your resonance to that Element lies—the closer to the rim, the greater the influence; the closer to the center, the weaker the influence. Once you've drawn a dot for each Element, connect them. The closer you come to drawing a circle, the more balanced the influence of the Elements; the more elliptical the shape, the more you need to focus on potential imbalances.

Too much fire? Maybe you have a tendency to burn through your money. Or maybe you spend it like water. Or you have it evaporate into the air. Perhaps, like a squirrel with a cache of tasty nuts, you bury your money in a secret place in your backyard. In Katherine's case, the financial planets of her astrological birth chart help to add some overall balance to her life; let's see now what these planets say about *your* Elemental abundance.

Astrology and Your Elemental Abundance

We are going to take a look at two astrological birth charts to see how the Elemental energies contribute to an individual's abundance. Once again we focus on the financial planets—Venus ♀, Mars ♂, Jupiter ♃, and Saturn ♄—to determine each person's Elemental Abundance Signature.

As you read, you'll want to refer to this table that matches up the signs of the Zodiac and the Elements.

Fire	Earth	Air	Water
Aries ♈	Taurus ♉	Gemini ♊	Cancer ♋
Leo ♌	Virgo ♍	Libra ♎	Scorpio ♏
Sagittarius ♐	Capricorn ♑	Aquarius ♒	Pisces ♓

Alan Greenspan, chairman of the Federal Reserve Bank and himself a multimillionaire, has successfully managed both his own finances and the finances of the United States. As chairman of the Federal Reserve Bank, he and his board set the interest rates at which banks lend money. A mere word from Greenspan can send stock prices soaring or cause them to plummet. Many commentators credit Greenspan and his ability to keep a cool head on his shoulders with preserving the strength of the U.S. economy and shoring up global markets during the late 1990s when Russia and Asia fell into financial crisis.

Have a look at Alan Greenspan's astrological birth chart. (Note that Greenspan's chart, like Warren Buffett's chart in Chapter 1, is a noon chart. So be aware that his Moon ☽ sign as shown here might not be completely accurate.) Take a moment to examine this chart and see what you notice about it.

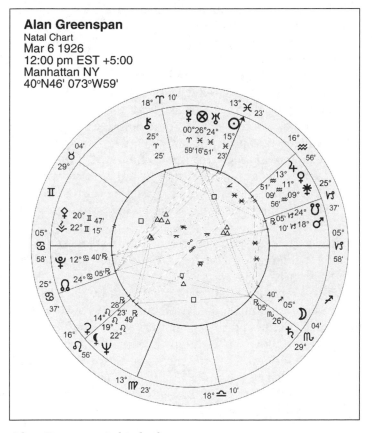

Alan Greenspan's birth chart.

To determine Greenspan's Elemental Abundance Signature, we noted in which sign each of his financial planets sits. Here is what we found.

Alan Greenspan's Elemental Abundance Signature

Financial Planets	Astro Sign	Element
Venus ♀	Aquarius ♒	Air
Mars ♂	Capricorn ♑	Earth
Jupiter ♃	Aquarius ♒	Air
Saturn ♄	Scorpio ♏	Water

Alan Greenspan has two financial planets in Air signs, one in an Earth sign, and one in a Water sign. None of the financial planets in Greenspan's birth chart sits in a Fire sign. The predominance of Air energy among Greenspan's financial planets indicates that he is able to take a rational approach to money and finances.

Greenspan has been associated with the conservative writer/philosopher Ayn Rand, author of *Atlas Shrugged* and proponent of a philosophy known as "objectivism." Some describe Rand as believing that selfishness is the best principle on which to run a society. The absence of Fire energy among Greenspan's financial planets and the predominance of Air would indicate that his take on material matters can seem cold and cerebral. And yet he does have a good balance with emotional Water and practical Earth keeping his head from drifting into the clouds.

As a contrast to Greenspan's conservative pin-stripe style, let's look at country singer Willie Nelson's birth chart and determine his Elemental Abundance Signature.

Nelson, if you remember, had his farm raided by the IRS in 1990. His lawyer and accountants had advised him to borrow a large sum of money to invest in cattle and thus gain a tax write-off. The only problem was the IRS did not allow the write-off. Eventually they came to Nelson with a bill for $30 million. To settle this debt, they took just about everything he owned. The lesson here? Be wary of your advisors and keep a watch on your own wallet! But let's look at the Elements and their energies in Willie Nelson's Elemental Abundance Signature.

Willie Nelson's Elemental Abundance Signature

Financial Planets	Astro Sign	Element
Venus ♀	Taurus ♉	Earth
Mars ♂	Virgo ♍	Earth
Jupiter ♃	Virgo ♍	Earth
Saturn ♄	Aquarius ♒	Air

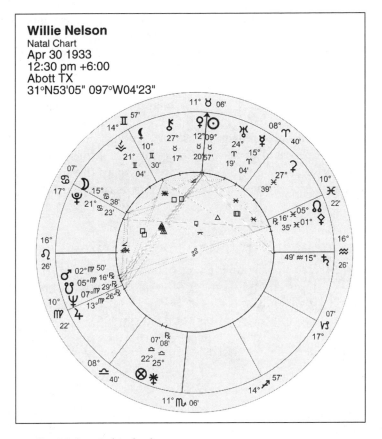

Willie Nelson's birth chart.

Earth, Earth, Earth, and Air! You may have noticed that all the Air and Fire signs of the Zodiac have *yang* energy, and all the Water and Earth signs have *yin* energy. So not only does Willie Nelson have an imbalance and a predominance of Earth among his financial planets, he also has energy tipped heavily toward *yin*. Perhaps this *yin* imbalance can explain his reliance on his advisors, who got him into such upsetting financial trouble.

Luckily for Willie, the combination of his Earthy Venus ♀ and cool, logical, and precise Mars ♂ have lent him artistic ability, drive, and a high degree of skill. Willie was able to pay the IRS back, and that same year he was elected to the Country Music Hall of Fame. His Jupiter ♃ in Virgo ♍ indicates success through perseverance, and Willie has persevered. This placement of Jupiter also values work and service to others—so it is no surprise that he helped to start Farm Aid, the series of benefit concerts devoted to bailing financially ailing farmers out of debt.

Just so you know where we are coming from, Katherine's financial planets map out to be Water, Water, Fire, and Earth. Although she does have a personal affinity for Air and that Element's mental machinations as you have seen in her Elemental Asset Allocation, her approach to financial issues does tend to be more emotional and intuitive rather than strictly rational. Arlene's financial planets map out to be Earth, Water, Fire, and Air! What can we say? Arlene is one sharp business-woman!

Your Elemental Abundance Signature

Now it's time to see how your Elements stack up. Get out your natal chart and fill in the sign and Element of your four financial planets. Refer to the chart of signs and Elements earlier in this chapter if you need help remembering the symbols for each sign.

Financial Planets	Astro Sign	Element
Venus ♀	_____	_____
Mars ♂	_____	_____
Jupiter ♃	_____	_____
Saturn ♄	_____	_____

Perhaps your Elemental Abundance Signature came out perfectly balanced like Arlene's. Maybe you tip toward rational and thoughtful Air, the way Alan Greenspan does. Or perhaps your Elemental Abundance signature emphasizes Water, the way Katherine's does, or Earth like Willie Nelson's. Now that you have seen the Elemental energies of your financial planets, you may gain a new understanding of your financial habits. Your Elemental Abundance Signature describes the Elemental tendencies of your natural energy.

Remember that an imbalance in these energies does not doom you to financial ruin. You still have free will. Knowing and understanding the energies that are natural to you can help you avoid pitfalls. If you know, for instance, that you can be overly Watery about your money and let it flow away from you in a bout of emotional spending, you also know that cashing your paycheck is not a good idea. Instead, you deposit it in the bank, an action that adds some Earth energy, stability, and security to your life. Understanding your own Elemental energy traits will also help you to make the best of what comes naturally to you so that you can act in your own best interest.

The Elemental Abundance Energy of the Day

When you do certain Tarot spreads, you pick a card from among the court cards (Kings, Queens, Knights, and Pages) of the Minor Arcana to represent you. Because each suit of the Minor Arcana corresponds directly to one of the Elements, you can also use the court cards to gauge the Elemental Abundance Energy of the day.

Separate out the 16 court cards of the Minor Arcana. If you have the time, take a few moments to examine these cards. See whether you are drawn to one card in particular. If so, ask yourself whether you feel that the card represents you and your energy. Or does the card you are focusing on represent the kind of energy that you want and feel is missing from your life?

Now shuffle all the court cards together. As you shuffle, think about your money and abundance issues. Ask the cards about the Elemental Abundance energy of the day. When you feel that you have shuffled enough and that the cards have an answer for you, cut the cards and deal one card from the top of the deck.

We just did, and this is what we got:

The Page of Wands has a fiery energy.

The Page of Wands, of course, is associated with the Element of Fire. All of the Pages are considered to be messengers who bear important information. This card indicates good news, so perhaps we should be expecting a phone call, fax, or e-mail informing us that we have landed that really cool project that's been on the back burner. The energy of the Page of Wands is one of enthusiasm. The Page himself loves to travel, especially to new and exotic places. Could this mean that our next project will take us on a business trip abroad? Now, wouldn't that be exciting!

What if you deal out a card that just seems to have nothing to do with what is going on with you and your money? Let's say you got the Page of Wands and you know that you aren't expecting any useful information regarding money or your finances. In such a situation, the card will be telling you what you need—some Fire! Some spunk! Some get up and go! Maybe planning a business trip, whether to Europe or just to the bank, could be just the thing to re-ignite your spark and get your passionate energies burning again.

If you haven't yet dealt yourself a card from the court cards to represent the Elemental Abundance energy of the day, do so now. Spend some time examining the card. Look at all the little details. Notice how the card makes you feel. Make some notes about your feelings if you are so moved. Now, focus on the card's meaning. Let your intuition and your heart guide you, as well as your head. Consider whether the card is showing you the existing energy of the day. Or perhaps it is trying to tell you what energy you need to achieve better Elemental and financial balance.

Often those two things are one and the same. If you can tap into the energy of the day, you can work with that energy and allow it to help you. If you get the Queen of Cups, for instance, the cards may be telling you that the path to abundance is through Water and your intuition, so you better go with the flow. The Queen of Swords, on the other hand, will tell you that your abundance on a given day will come through thought, ideas, and mental inventiveness. The Knight of Pentacles will show you the way to prosperity through work, honesty, and a job well done.

If you would like a reading of the day's Elemental energy with more nuances, deal out four cards. If you get two or more cards in one suit, you'll know that the predominant suit represents the strongest Elemental energy of the day, while the others will add their own power to the mix. Your new intuitive understanding of the Elements helps you create your personal Elemental energy balance sheet of each day's abundance potential.

chapter 4

Attracting the Wealth You Want

Assess your wealth
Basic Business Astrology
Moon magic in Astrology's houses
Charting events
Tarot's Horoscope Spread: Your financial year
Change your focus: Nurturing self-talk

Money, money, money, money. As a culture, we worry about it, obsess over it, spend it, and even sing about it. Of course, there is more to wealth than just money. We show you how to define your own personal wealth and which areas of your life you need to work on to achieve true abundance. We take a look at the Moon and some basics from Business Astrology to help get you and your business on a good financial footing. You learn how to work with the Moon energy of a given day instead of against it. Plus, you use the Tarot to do some financial forecasting of your own. Attracting the wealth you want does take effort, but using the Intuitive Arts of Astrology, Tarot, and Psychic Intuition can help you and make this work profitable and fun.

Different Kinds of Wealth

When we talk about wealth, we are not just talking about money. You can have a wealth of friends and loving relationships, a wealth of time, artistic wealth, or spiritual wealth. It's easy to get hung up on monetary wealth because it is concrete and easier to define than wealth's other forms. More money is seen as good. And working all the time to attain money is seen as virtuous. But at what price? If you have to work 70 hours a week to bring home that large paycheck and never get to see your friends or family and never get to have fun, is it really worth it? It may be, or it may be for now, but ultimately you may decide that you want some more time to yourself—time to devote to relationships, artistic pursuits, spiritual practice, or just plain goofing off.

It can be tricky to achieve the right balance (there's that word again!) between all the areas of your life; with some thought about your real needs and desires, however, you can achieve the mix that is right for you. You can use Astrology, Tarot, and your Psychic Intuition to help you identify your real needs and wants. You can also use these Intuitive Arts to help you strike a nice balance. Why strive for this balance? Balance breeds abundance!

Your Piece(s) of the Pie

Remember your Elemental Asset Allocation from the previous chapter? Well, you're going to use your Psychic Intuition to help you draw another pie chart. This one represents the different areas of wealth in your life and how satisfied you feel with each one. Map out your own personal wealth.

Each line in the figure represents a different area of your life: money, family/friends, fun/art, and spirituality. Place a dot on each line to indicate how satisfied you are with that area of your life. If you are totally satisfied in a given area, place your dot on the edge of the circle. If you are almost satisfied, place your dot a bit inside the circle. If you feel that you are totally lacking in this area, place your dot near the center of the circle.

Once you have graphed all your dots, connect them. Ideally, you want to come out with another circle. This circle would indicate that your wealth is balanced and that you have achieved your abundance—what we all want! Probably your figure will come out lopsided. The deflated areas of your circle indicate the areas in your life that need a little extra wealth of your attention!

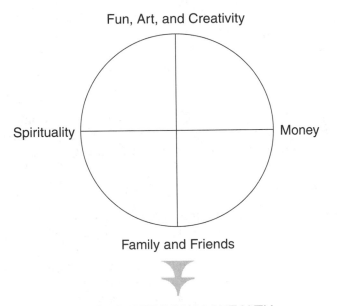

YOUR PERSONAL WEALTH

Your wealth in four of its forms.

Business 101

Maybe what you want *really* is money—cold hard cash. We are going to look at some principles from Business Astrology to help you get what you want. Know, too, that you can use these same ideas to help you attain wealth in the other, nonmonetary, areas of your life as well.

We've talked quite a bit in the previous chapters about the planets Venus ♀, Mars ♂, Saturn ♄, and Jupiter ♃. We looked at these planets in your birth chart and in the charts of others. Our focus has been on the astrological energies that help to form your personality. We also need to look at the astrological energies that are present on a given day. You may have a lot of Fiery Aries ♈ energy in your birth chart, but the energy of the day may be one of calm and practical Taurus ♉.

In Business Astrology you can look at birth charts, which indicate the energies present at the date, time, and place of your birth. You also look at event charts. An event chart is just like a birth chart, but it examines an event, such as the incorporation of a company, the signing of legal documents, or the first meeting with a business associate. In a sense, all of these events are births. What all of these charts show is the position of the heavenly bodies at the precise place and moment something or someone has come into being.

Planning with Astrology in mind can save you from major headaches down the road. Using Business Astrology, you can help to form the character of your future enterprises and ensure their success. Unlike your birthday, over which you had little control, you can choose exactly when you are going to meet with your lawyer to sign papers to incorporate your company. Picking a day when the astrological energies present are conducive to business will help abundance flourish.

Phases of the Moon

The simplest astrological way of looking at the energy of the day is by studying the Moon ☽. Although the Moon is not really a planet, its energy has a big impact on all of us on Earth. Surely you have felt the lunatic energy of the Full Moon, which can cause dogs to howl and people to act strange. The phases of the Moon—the New Moon, First Quarter, Full Moon, and Last Quarter—can impact you and your financial plans and projects.

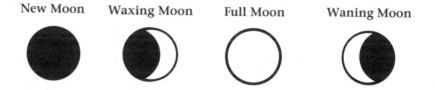

| New Moon | Waxing Moon | Full Moon | Waning Moon |

The Moon takes 29½ days to move through its cycle—from New to Quarter to Full and back again. As you might expect, the New Moon is full of new energy. This is a great time to start new projects and get the ball rolling on your latest financial plan. Under a First Quarter Moon, you and your new enterprise may experience challenges. People you are working for may question your plan, even though it is already underway, or they may hold up your work and question you about your motives. If you know to expect the challenges of the First Quarter Moon, you will be prepared and easily rise to meet them.

The Full Moon is the time of the Moon's greatest energy and brightness. Under this bright Moon, you will be able to accurately see how your investment project is fairing. This can be a time of joy in your achievements. Or it can be a time of disillusionment when you see how much your profit has veered away from your projection. If you have been working with the phases of the Moon, though, you should be able to reap your rewards at this time. The Last Quarter Moon is a time of assessment and learning. This is the time for you to look back over your profit or loss, see what you could have done differently, and learn from your past actions.

Many calendars note the phases of the Moon, so even if you cannot see it, you can keep track of where the Moon is in its cycle. You can also find this information online at *The Old Farmer's Almanac* site (www.almanac.com). When planning any financial business—a meeting, signing of contracts, beginning a new project—in addition to paying attention to the phase of the Moon (New, First Quarter, Full, or Last Quarter), you want to look at what astrological sign the Moon is in.

Moon Sign Abundance

Because the Moon ☽ travels around the Earth quickly, the Moon passes through all the signs of the Zodiac every month. In a given month, the Moon spends two and a half days in each astrological sign. Each sign the Moon passes through has a different energy, and that vibe affects you and your abundance.

The days that the Moon ☽ is in the same sign as your natal Sun ☉ sign are known as your Lunar High. For example, if you are a Virgo ♍, you will feel your best and get a lot of energy from the Moon when it is in Virgo. Conversely, your Lunar Low is the time of the month when the Moon is in the sign opposite your natal Sun sign. If you are a Virgo, you will feel as if the energy all around you is just rubbing you the wrong way when the Moon is in Pisces ☽ ♓. So you see how important the Moon can be! This is not to say that anything bad will happen to you during your Lunar Low. It just might not be your favorite time of the month! Here's a table that shows the signs of the Zodiac and their opposites:

Astro Signs and Their Opposites

Aries ♈	Libra ♎
Taurus ♉	Scorpio ♏
Gemini ♊	Sagittarius ♐
Cancer ♋	Capricorn ♑
Leo ♌	Aquarius ♒
Virgo ♍	Pisces ♓

If you know the Moon's sign on a given day, you can plan your affairs so that lunar energy aids you and works for you in all of your endeavors. An astrological calendar will show you the Moon's sign. Keep in mind that you have only one Lunar Low per month, and it only lasts about two days. The rest of the month—which is most of the time!—the world can be your oyster. Let's take a trip through all the signs of the Zodiac and see what kind of energy the Moon in each sign brings to help navigate the lunar cycle.

Moon in Aries ☽ ♈: Go!

When the Moon is in Aries, you want to start new things. An Aries Moon promotes initiative, energy, and ideas. This is also a great time for you to tap into the energy of leadership and willpower. The days that the Moon is in Aries are full of general get-up-and-go. If your natal Sun ☉ sign is Aries, this is a particularly energy-filled few days for you. The energy all around you is in synch with your natural natal energy. So get out there and make that deal, sign that contract, or launch your new product. You Libras ♎, on the other hand, may want to lay low and rest.

Moon in Taurus ☽ ♉: Steady

When the Moon is in Taurus, the vibe is one of dependability and harmony. The energy of the Taurus Moon is also about money and material goods (and love). Because Taurus has *yin* energy, you might want to meditate on issues involving your prosperity during this time. If your natal Sun ☉ sign is Taurus, you will feel full of vim and vigor during this period, and you will find this a good time to begin work on sorting out your finances. If, on the other hand, you were born under the sign of Scorpio ♏, you may want to take these couple of days off.

Moon in Gemini ☽ ♊: Communicate

Under a Gemini Moon, the energy is one of communication. This is a great time to write, write, and write some more. So pull out that old business plan that you have hidden away in a drawer, and get to it. Verbal communications are also enhanced under a Gemini Moon, and Gemini energy is conducive to travel, too. Need to travel to make a speech to pitch a new product? This could be the time to do just that. If your natal Sun ☉ sign is Gemini, you'll be feeling great at this time of the month. You may want to delve into your business correspondence or, hey, whatever happened to that novel you started? For those of you born with a Sagittarius Sun ♐ ☉, take a break and know that your day (and its Sagi energy!) will come.

Moon in Cancer ☽ ♋: Feel

The energy under a Cancer Moon is *yin* and tends toward both the emotional and the nurturing. This is a good time for working on issues regarding your home and your domestic finances. You also may want to deal with any emotional issues that you have regarding your home and home finances—just be aware that your emotions could run high. Cancer, of course, is ruled by the Moon; so with the Moon in Cancer, we get a strong dose of lunar energy. If your natal Sun ☉ sign is Cancer, you'll probably be ready to start new things at this time of the month. Perhaps you'll have the energy to look into refinancing your home, or maybe you will start looking for a new place to live. All you Capricorns ♑ out there may find it best to slow down, smell the roses, and wait for the Moon to move on to its next sign.

Moon in Leo ☽ ♌: Courage

A Leo Moon brings feelings of courage, bravery, and the energy of the lion. This is also a time for showmanship, acting, and exerting your will over others. As such, this would be a great time to make a presentation regarding money. You will be engaging, fun to watch, and very persuasive. Or you could use this bold Leo energy to ask for that raise you've been thinking about. You will be able to use Leo energy to help present and promote an important product—yourself. All you Leos will be full of lion energy and ready to charm your way into getting exactly what you want. For those of you born with a natal Sun in Aquarius ☉ ♒, you may want to spend the next day or two being mellow and laying low.

Moon in Virgo ☽ ♍: Details

The energy of the Virgo Moon is concerned with matters of the intellect, employment, health, and, of course, details. This is a great time to read contracts and go over everything with a fine-toothed comb. There's also a vibe of self-improvement in the atmosphere, which you may want to use to correct any accounting bad habits, or examine your spending pattern; or you could use this energy to look for a job higher up on the corporate ladder. All you Virgos will feel particularly sharp during the Virgo Moon, but those born under a Pisces Sun ♓ ☉ will want to kick back—maybe in a nice heated pool.

Moon in Libra ☽ ♎: Balance

Under a Libra Moon, the energies that surround you are conducive to balance—emotional, intellectual, and financial. This energy is also good for issues concerning justice, the seeking of harmony or beauty, and all things social. Libra energy has a great deal of charm, so perhaps you will want to harness that force to help you organize a social event for work, a fundraising party for an art museum, or a benefit to help cover a friend's legal expenses. If you were born under the Sun ☉ sign of Libra, this is your time of the month to shine. If your Sun sign is Aries ♈, you may want to take a break till all this foreign Libra energy dies down.

Moon in Scorpio ☽ ♏: Intensity

The Scorpio Moon brings intensity to everything. The energy of the Scorpio Moon highlights transformation, desire, and issues of power. This is a good time to work on making real changes in your life that will move you toward getting what you really want. This is also a great time to harness some penetrating Scorpio energy to try to see beneath the surface of a boss or a colleague at work. You can also tap into your intuition during these few days of the month to see below your psychic surface and use the knowledge that you gain to help you grow and change. Those of you born under a natal Scorpio Sun ♏ ☉ will revel in this period of time. Use your natural Scorpio energy well and you can regenerate yourself and your sense of abundance. For those of you born with a natal Sun in Taurus ☉ ♉, let your natural steadiness be a comfort to you and take these few days off.

Moon in Sagittarius ☽ ♐: Enthusiasm

When the Moon is in Sagittarius, you will have lots of energy to explore and search for information. The Sagittarius vibe is one of enthusiasm, optimism, high spirits, and fun. You may want to use this energy for ferreting out the truth, which often involves some serious digging. This is also a good time for you to turn your attention to work that concerns legal matters or publishing. If you were born under a natal Sagittarius

70

Sun ♐ ☉, you will love these times of the month. Why not harness your high spirits to get cracking on your new moneymaking enterprise? For those of you born with a natal Sun in Gemini ♊, wait a day or two till the energy of the world is more in sync with your own.

Moon in Capricorn ☽ ♑: Achievement

The Moon in Capricorn is a practical achievement-oriented Moon. This energy is associated with careers, discipline, determination, recognition, and success. So this would be a great time to use some of the Capricorn energy in the atmosphere to organize your life and your financial papers so you can be a success. If you were born with a natal Capricorn Sun ♑ ☉, you will love this time of the month and be able to squeeze every last drop of mountain-climbing Capricorn energy out of these days. For those of you with a Cancer Sun ♋ ☉ sign, everyone is marching to a beat that you just don't understand. So take a break and know that soon the energy of the day will belong to you.

Moon in Aquarius ☽ ♒: Revolution

Under an Aquarius Moon, you'll feel the revolutionary energy of that sign in the air. This is a great time for work that involves freedom, creative expression, or problem solving. This is also a good time to cultivate your extrasensory abilities and friendships. Perhaps you will want to harness your psychic energies to solve a financial problem. You may even want to get together with a group of friends to brainstorm some ideas. Those of you born under a natal Aquarius Sun ♒ ☉ will feel the enhancement of your natural energies. Use these energies to find creative solutions that will guarantee your financial freedom. If you were born under the Sun sign of Leo ♌, take it easy for now and know that the Moon will soon be in a new sign.

Moon in Pisces ☽ ♓: Compassion

The Pisces Moon brings an energy of compassion. So this can be a good time for healing. Pisces is also concerned with imagination, dreams, and intuition. You could hook into this vibe and use your Psychic Intuition to help heal your relationship to money and your sense of abundance. Or maybe your dreams will bring you a vision that lays out what you need to do to heal. If you were born under the natal Sun ☉ sign of Pisces ♓, the world will be marching to your fishy beat.

So make sure you use and enjoy this time of the month. For those of you born under the Sun sign of Virgo ♍, wait, mellow out, chill, because your day will come.

Void of Course Moon

As the Moon travels around the Earth through each sign of the Zodiac, it "goes void" as it moves from one sign to another. During this time, it's as if the Moon were in a tunnel. Much the way that you just get a lot of static when your car radio is on and you drive through a tunnel, the Moon's energies don't do what they usually do. The void of course Moon, or Moon void, period is best for nonmaterial, *yin* activities, such as meditation, prayer, psychotherapy, sleep, or yoga. (Or loafing around!)

The void Moon is not a good time to start on a new project or plan of action. It's also not a good time to make decisions, start a business, or buy things. Articles purchased during the void of course Moon often fail to fulfill their purpose. Actions inaugurated also do not manifest with the expected abundant result. You can find information on the timing of Moon void periods in an astrological calendar. Or check out www.artcharts.com and click on the link for Moon voids.

A Good Decision

Now that you know a lot about the Moon ☽ and a little bit more about Business Astrology, let's take a look at a business decision that has reaped huge rewards for the people involved.

Country singer Shania Twain has had the good fortune (actually, we think it is more than just luck) to win five Grammy Awards and an Academy of Country Music Entertainer of the Year Award. On top of those accolades, she has been named the top-selling artists of the decade by Nielsen Soundscan, a music-industry database that counts each album sold nationwide. By early 2003, her album *Come on Over* had sold 19 million copies. These sales figures have earned the disc the status of best-selling album by a woman—ever. And Shania herself was ranked number 7 on the list of the "40 Greatest Women of Country Music" put out by Country Music Television.

Let's look at the event chart for the release of Shania's album *Come on Over*. If it helps, think of this as the birth chart of the album and see how its personality and success have been shaped by the stars.

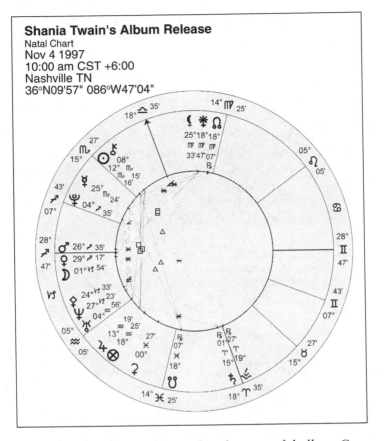

The sky when Shania Twain's hugely successful album Come on Over *was released.*

You will notice that the Moon is in Capricorn ☽ ♑, indicating achievement, recognition, and success. Note, too, that Venus ♀, which is on the horizon and about to rise, is in Sagittarius ♐, the sign of enthusiasm, optimism, publishing, and fun. In a person's chart, Venus in Sagittarius ♀ ♐ is usually the mark of someone who has a lot of friends, and we would say that this is true of this album, too—19 million friends, to date! Mars ♂ is also sharing in the optimistic Sagittarius ♐ energy, and Jupiter in Aquarius ♃ ♒ finds its fortune through the people that it meets, which in this case would be the music-buying public. Saturn is in Aries ♄ ♈ and is retrograde, which means that it appears to be moving backward in the sky. (We talk about retrogrades and what they mean in a later chapter.) The placement of Saturn, the planet associated with limits, in Aries, a sign associated with freedom and breaking through limitations, would indicate the breakaway nature of this album's success. This placement, too, describes persistence, a trait this album exhibits in its sales figures. It came out in 1997 and, at the time of this writing in 2003, it continues to sell.

Astrologers look at many other factors when picking a good day to transact business. We will get into more of this information later in the book. For now, though, take a look at the relationship between all of the planets in this chart. Notice that Venus ♀ and Mars ♂ sit very close together. So here, Mars ♂, the planet of action, which is crucial to business, is giving energy to Venus ♀, the planet associated with money and physical attractiveness, among other things. What this equation adds up to is one moneymaking album with sex appeal!

You can assess the power of the financial planets by obtaining an event chart for an important moment in *your* life—the day you passed the bar exam or cashed the check for publication of your first short story.

Now look back to the chart of Shania's album release. Find the Moon ☽ and notice what house it is in. Remember we said her album's Moon is in Capricorn ☽ ♑, the sign of achievement. Now we can add another piece to the equation—Moon in Capricorn in the 1st house. The 1st house is the area of your physical self, self-image, personality, and identity. The Moon ☽ in the 1st house indicates a desire to be admired and appreciated. A 1st house Moon is also all about imaginative self-expression. When you add it all up, you get success in imaginative expression and achievement in attaining admiration!

Each astrological house represents an area of the sky at the time of birth. Imagine that the circle in the center of the chart is the Earth. The horizontal line that divides the pie in half is the horizon. Everything above the horizon was visible in the sky at the hour of your birth. Although the planets below the horizon could not be seen, they are still important in defining the unique energy the birth chart reveals. As you can see, the houses are numbered starting on the left below the horizon line and moving counterclockwise.

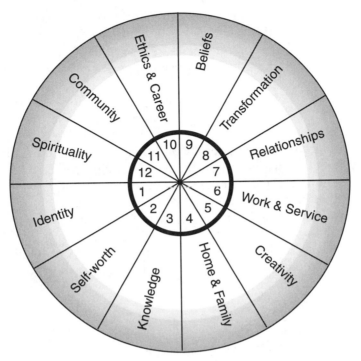

The 12 houses.

Here is a list of keywords associated with each house.

House	Keywords
1st	Physical self, personality, identity, early childhood
2nd	Possessions, earning abilities, self-esteem
3rd	Knowledge, communication, siblings, environment
4th	Home, family, foundation of life
5th	Creativity, risk, fun, romance, children
6th	Personal responsibilities, health, work, service
7th	Primary relationships, partnerships
8th	Joint resources, sex, death, transformation, and rebirth
9th	Education, travel, philosophy, ideals, religion, law
10th	Reputation, career, social responsibilities
11th	Goals, groups, friends
12th	Subconscious, karma, privacy, psychic vision

Now take a look at your own astrological birth or event chart. Find your Moon ☽ and make a note of which house it is in. Here's a brief rundown of what the Moon indicates in each of the 12 houses.

The Moon ☽ in the 1st house: Imaginative self-expression, desire to be admired and appreciated

The Moon ☽ in the 2nd house: Ability to earn money through contacts with women, food, and real estate; emotional security tied to possessions

The Moon ☽ in the 3rd house: Concern about siblings, education, and travel; highly imaginative and curious; strong memory skills

The Moon ☽ in the 4th house: Strong devotion to home and family, particularly to the mother

The Moon ☽ in the 5th house: Love of pleasure; romantic; creative; strong desire for children

The Moon ☽ in the 6th house: Great sense of responsibility and consideration of others; enjoys work in service areas, especially having to do with food; emotions tied closely to job and work; may change jobs often

The Moon ☽ in the 7th house: Popular, sensitive, responsive to needs of others; partners—in business and marriage—tend to be moody; importance of domestic and emotional security

The Moon ☽ in the 8th house: Psychic ability; interested in issues involving death and rebirth; need for security; strong instinct with regard to the needs of others; relation to money, particularly to shared resources, can be changeable; possible inheritance, especially through the mother

The Moon ☽ in the 9th house: Love of travel and holistic learning; strong ties to religious or philosophical beliefs; imaginative and receptive mind; teaching ability; openness to the supernatural

The Moon ☽ in the 10th house: Careers that deal with the public, especially marketing, buying and selling of commodities, and the shipping industry; strong drive for achievement; desire for success linked to the welfare of the public

The Moon ☽ in the 11th house: Emotionally intuitive; goals involving groups, especially of friends; strong attachment to friends, many of whom may be women

The Moon ☽ in the 12th house: Sensitive, receptive, and intuitive; need for alone time; creative imagination; abilities in the many areas of counseling

We talk more about the planets in the houses (and the signs in the houses) and what they mean in later chapters.

Your Financial Year in the Cards

To get a general view of your financial year ahead, you can do a Horoscope Spread. As you have seen, your birth chart is divided up into 12 houses, each of which relates to a different area of your life. You can use the idea of the houses and place 12 cards, 1 card in each house, in a circle. Each card will represent one month of the year.

When you are ready to do your Horoscope Spread, shuffle the cards and think about your financial year. Divide the deck into three stacks, and then pick one of the stacks. Deal out the top 12 cards, starting by placing your first card in the first house and working counterclockwise around the circle. The first card you deal represents what the next month will bring. The second card shows what you should expect in the next two months, the third card what you should expect in the next three months, and so on around the circle.

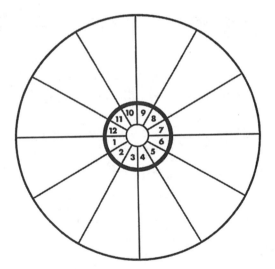

Tarot's Horoscope Spread.

Spend some time looking at the cards and get a feeling for what they are saying. Then write down the date that you do your reading and your interpretation of each card in the space provided. It's important to record the date of a long-term reading such as this one, because without it, you will lose track of which card represents which month.

Date of reading: _____

Card 1. In the next month, _____

Card 2. In the next 2 months, _____

Card 3. In the next 3 months, _____

Card 4. In the next 4 months, _____

Card 5. In the next 5 months, _____

Card 6. In the next 6 months, _____

Card 7. In the next 7 months, _____

Card 8. In the next 8 months, _____

Card 9. In the next 9 months, _____

Card 10. In the next 10 months, _____

Card 11. In the next 11 months, _____

Card 12. In the next 12 months, _____

Check back and look at this reading every few months. You might be amazed at your reading's accuracy. Over time you may start to see things in the cards you missed the first time around.

Talk, Talk, Talk: Your Psyche, Your Money, and You

You have done all the right things. You consult the Tarot, examine your astrological birth chart, and check the stars before making big financial decisions, but you still find yourself constantly broke and struggling to attract the wealth you want. It could be that you are a victim of your own negative thinking.

As Lynn Robinson, writer and intuition expert, has written, "If you want something a great deal (prosperity) and hold positive thoughts and feelings about it, you will attract it into your life. If you don't want something (poverty) and constantly feel fear and anxiety about it, you will attract it into your life. Whatever you put your focus on begins a process of manifestation. Think about something—positive or negative—with enough strong intent and emotion, and you will have it in your life." Lynn points out that she herself had just these kinds of problems.

At the time, she was working with affirmations, such as "I am prosperous" or "I am a magnet to money," but she was still broke. Then she began to examine her inner dialogue, the things that she was saying to herself as she went about her day-to-day life. She discovered that when she wasn't writing out her affirmations she was constantly dwelling on the negative, imagining financial catastrophes.

Pay close attention to what you tell yourself as you go about your day. When you catch yourself having a negative anxious fantasy about, say, your car being repossessed, change the channel! Force yourself to imagine something else, something positive. Maybe you can focus on images of washing your car and the feelings of pride that its shiny surface evokes. Or imagine having your car professionally detailed and how nice it will be to have it be all spic-and-span.

Or carry the Moon card from your Tarot deck with you. Whenever you have a negative thought or feel anxious about your finances, gaze at the Moon card and remember that the wildness of the wolf is balanced out by the tameness of the dog. Notice the face of the Moon herself and her serene energy. Feel the temptation to dip into wild negativity, but choose to allow yourself to settle into equilibrium and the natural balance of these two forces that rests inside us all.

Feel the balance between the wild and the tame.

If you spend much of your time thinking that the worst will happen, you are going to attract those bad things to you even if you are using positive affirmations. Before the affirmations can help you, you have to work on changing your self-talk. Otherwise, an affirmation such as "I am a millionaire" will act like a Band-Aid used to heal a broken leg; it won't do a thing! In fact, as Lynn points out, if you have a huge gap between the affirmations that you are using and the thoughts that you dwell on normally, you could very well cause your inner self to reject the positive statement altogether. While you are working to break yourself of the bad habit of negative self talk, try using simple positive affirmations such as "Everything is okay."

If negative self-talk is a big problem for you (or if you are simply interested in learning more about using your intuition), check out Lynn Robinson's website at www.lynnrobinson.com for more of her really smart ideas. You also may want to carry your Intuitive Arts notebook around with you for a few days. Note your negative thoughts. You can use these negative thoughts to create your own personalized affirmations. For example, if you frequently say to yourself "I am so broke," replace that thought with "I am learning about abundance and opening to it more and more every day."

chapter 5

Neither a Lender Nor a Borrower Be ...

Your true location in relation to abundance
Assessing your assets
Let the Tarot help you learn your lessons
Astrology's aspects of your financial personality
Synastry: The Astrology of relationships

We're going to take a cold hard look at your financial situation and your relationship to money in the present day. Where are you right now? Perhaps you are frugal and hoard your resources and cash. Or you are generous and give away what you get. Maybe you are always strapped and looking for help from your relatives, friends, co-workers, or boss. Or maybe you are the quiet millionaire next door. Perhaps you like to gamble or take high-flying stock market risks. Or you stuff all your cash into your mattress and hope for the best. We're going to examine your money psychology with an eye to your own future happiness. Are you satisfied with your feelings and behavior around money issues? Does your financial style match your own image of yourself? Does it match your life partner's money style? Let's use Astrology, Tarot, and your Psychic Intuition to explore your orientation to money in the present day.

"X" Marks the Spot

Right now, where are you financially and how do you feel about it? It's important to define precisely where you are before you start moving toward where you want to go. Not too long ago, a friend of ours had to drive to an event in a city she'd never been to. She'd printed out directions and a map from the Internet, but she missed her exit off the highway. She pulled over, looked at her map, and couldn't locate where she was in relationship to the map. She kept driving in what she hoped was the right direction. She drove and drove. She drove in circles. Eventually she got directions, but she was more than an hour late reaching her destination. Having a map that shows your destination probably won't help you much if you don't know where you are or if you are not even on the map to begin with. To find yourself on the financial map, you need to be aware.

As psychologists always say, awareness is the first step in any process of change. You first must become aware of your financial habits, your feelings about money, and your feelings about your financial situation. Your second step in the process of change is acceptance. You must accept what is. Beating yourself up or yelling at yourself for spending foolishly or wallowing in envy will not help you to reach your goals. Treating yourself harshly could very well propel you to indulge in more negative behavior. For example, you might feel angry at yourself and frustrated for blowing your weekly budget plan by buying this amazing pair of shoes or must-have kitchen gadget that you saw in a shop window. If you go on to berate yourself for your lack of self-control, you will succeed in making yourself feel bad. You also very well may go out and shop again to try to relieve yourself of the bad feeling. So treat yourself gently! Look at yourself with compassion and understanding. Once you have truly accepted your own behaviors and feelings, you can move into action.

But let's back up a little bit and identify exactly where you are right now in the present moment. Becoming aware of your true situation is most illuminating, and it can be fun. Really. Check out these two exercises and see for yourself.

Pick a Card

Pull out these 10 Tarot cards: 4 of Wands, 2 of Pentacles, 4 of Pentacles, 7 of Cups, 7 of Swords, 10 of Wands, 8 of Swords, 9 of Swords, 5 of Wands, and 10 of Swords; and line them up in this order. Or study the black-and-white images printed here.

Which Tarot card represents your feelings about your finances, right now in the present day?

Which card represents your feelings about your finances, right now in the present moment? Don't think about this too much. Listen to your gut and allow your Psychic Intuition to guide you. Pick out the card that you feel best represents you and your feelings with regard to your financial situation. Spend some time studying the image on your card before you read on. How does the card make you feel? In your notebook, take a few minutes to write about what the card brings up for you.

Now let's take a look at each card and what it says about where you are in relation to your own personal abundance.

4 of Wands. Things in your life look and feel good. Your vibe right now is one of celebration. You have worked hard, and now you have the opportunity to enjoy your own abundance.

2 of Pentacles. Like the young man in the card, you are able to keep your funds in balance. You also are able to handle your feelings with regard to your finances. Sure, this takes some work on your part, but your lighthearted attitude helps you keep all your balls in the air.

4 of Pentacles. While your finances have a firm foundation, you are holding tightly to what you possess. Perhaps, like many people, you are afraid of losing what you have worked hard to attain. Could it be that loosening your grip a bit would give you more of an opportunity to enjoy what you already have?

7 of Cups. This card depicts a number of mysterious and fantastic beings. Perhaps you feel that the state of your finances is a mystery. Or are you busy looking at a fantasy version of your life instead of dealing with the real thing?

7 of Swords. There's a sneaky vibe to this card. If you picked this one, perhaps you feel that you are getting away with something. Or maybe you or someone close to you is indulging in secret spending. Perhaps you (or your partner) have secret credit card debt that you have been hiding.

10 of Wands. The man in this card is shouldering what looks to be a heavy burden. Perhaps you have taken on too many responsibilities— your own and those of the other people in your life as well. This card asks you to consider if you haven't taken on too much. Perhaps you can let go of one task or responsibility and lighten your load a bit.

8 of Swords. The woman in this card is imprisoned by her fear. Notice that the swords here are not touching her, and she is not being physically harmed in any way. This brings to mind Franklin Delano Roosevelt's words: "The only thing we have to fear is fear itself." Many, many people are trapped by their own financial fears. If financial fear is locking you up, know that you have the power to walk away from it, and you have already taken your first steps—by reading this book!

9 of Swords. This card is known as the "Nightmare card." In a reading, this card represents the loss of hope, bad dreams, and nightmares. Despair and anxiety are also a big part of this picture. We like to remind ourselves that nightmares aren't real. Certainly your feelings are real, but you can always work on changing them, and, as in the previous card description, you have already begun that process of change. So congratulate yourself on your bravery!

5 of Wands. Here we see discord and struggle. This card also indicates competitive action, but in an unfocused and disorganized form. A sense of confusion, agitation, and stress pervades this card. Perhaps financial fears and worries have been causing you to fight with your family or loved ones. You may need some good financial or legal advice to help everything (and everyone) in your life settle down.

10 of Swords. Wow, we hope you don't feel this way! But if you do feel as if your financial situation is killing you, know that this card represents the end of a cycle. The conditions that were "killing" you will come to an end. Your past obligations are now wrapping up. You are on the threshold of being reborn into a new karmic cycle.

We've noticed that many people, even those who seem calm and easy-going, harbor a lot of fear when it comes to their finances. But we are going to forge onward. Let's look at where you are and how you got there, all the while keeping an eye on your future abundance.

Your Personal Treasure Map

Do you really know where you are financially? Do you know where you are going? Using your Psychic Intuition, you are going to map out where you are in relationship to your abundance. You can use this map to remind yourself of your past accomplishments, inspire yourself, and keep yourself headed in the right direction.

You need a large sheet of paper or poster board and a clear surface on which to work. You also need:

- Colored pens and pencils
- Crayons
- Images from magazines
- Postcards
- Photographs
- A glue stick
- Yarn or string
- Sand or pebbles

Starting in the middle of your paper, draw or collage an image to represent you in the present moment and how you relate to your finances. Your representation of yourself does not have to actually look like you. You can use a symbol or draw something abstract that captures your present situation and how you feel about it. Or you could use an image from the Tarot.

Now draw a line that represents the path to your past. Put down three or four life events on your path that have led you to where you are now. You may want to make an image to represent your first paying job, opening your first savings account, getting your first credit card, buying a new home, a promotion at work, a marriage, or a divorce.

Next to each event image, make a symbol that represents your level of financial health. If you were broke, you may want to draw a big fat zero. If you were loaded, you could draw $$$$. Use your imagination and your Psychic Intuition here, and draw what feels right to you.

Once you have marked each event with a symbol that represents the state of your finances, think back on each individual event and the phase that it represents in your life. How did you feel about your situation? Did you feel stable, strapped, impoverished, or abundant? Next to each financial health symbol, place a symbol that represents how you felt about your abundance at the time. You could draw or collage a smiley face, a frown, a flourishing green plant, or anything that your Psychic Intuition comes up with that represents your feelings at the time.

Note that your feelings might not match the state of your checkbook. You may have felt happy and confident in relation to your abundance, but had very little actual cash. In such a case, you may want to draw a big fat zero, representing the relative lack of cold hard cash, next to a smiley face—your feelings of happiness and ease. Or you could have been fine financially but spent much of your time plagued by fear and worry. If your feelings about your abundance and your rational measurement of where you were financially never seem to go together, pay careful attention. Perhaps you think you need more money than you actually do. Perhaps having money is not the thing that is going to make you feel better. Perhaps the thing that you are seeking lies not in financial but in another form of abundance. Or perhaps examining your fears and where they really come from could help you better enjoy your life and all that you have. If these types of issues come up for you, spend some time writing about them in your notebook.

Let the images from your past help you to see your present and your future. If you have faced financial hardship in the past, give yourself a pat on the back for having gotten through it. Remember that you have survived, and perhaps even thrived, in the past, and you will continue to do so in the future.

Now you are ready to move on to the second part of this exercise. First put away the art supplies that you have just been using. Keep your map on your desk, or hang it over your workspace so that you can see it as you move into this second phase. Take a deep breath and get out your bank and credit card statements for the last year. Grab your calculator, some paper, and a pen. If you're feeling anxious, don't worry, and know that you are not alone in this. As finance guru Suze Orman has pointed out in her best-selling (and super helpful) book

The 9 Steps to Financial Freedom: Practical & Spiritual Steps So You Can Stop Worrying (Three Rivers Press, 2000), when it comes to money most people are afraid. And this fear prevents them from truly looking at and assessing their financial conditions. In this case, what you don't know (or are afraid to look at) can hurt you! So take a few deep breaths. Glance at your treasure map collage for reinforcement; now dive in and find the answers to these questions:

1. How much money do you really spend per month? How much per year?
2. Are you in debt? Is your debt growing?
3. Are you putting any money away in savings? How much per month? How much per year?
4. What is your monthly income? And how much is your yearly income?

After completing this exercise, you will know where you are right now in terms of actual numbers and with regard to your feelings. You must look at what truly is before you can start moving toward what you want. Perhaps you spend profligately. Or maybe you hoard all of your resources. Chances are that you fall somewhere between these two extremes. Once you know where you are, you can focus on how to make the best of your actual situation and from that vantage point you can begin to move toward your own abundance.

History Repeats Itself

You may have found, while reading the earlier sections of this chapter and doing the exercises, that history repeats itself. More specifically, you may have found that *your* history repeats: You keep finding yourself in the same financial situation again and again. It could be that karma is trying to teach you something. The lessons we need to learn from money often are intimately connected to the lessons we need to learn about life. To get some more clarity on what your lessons are in the present day, why not ask the Tarot what your lessons are? Afterward, you can use your Psychic Intuition to help you learn your lessons and move on.

You can use a Karmic Spread to discover your life (and your money) lessons. This easy four-card spread can help you discover why you seem to wind up in the same types of situations over and over again. The question you ask the cards when doing a Karmic Spread is always the same: *"What are the karmic lessons I am learning now?"* The key word here is "now," as our karmic lessons change as we acknowledge them, learn, and grow.

Think about your karmic lessons and ask the question, while you shuffle your Tarot deck. Then, if you like, cut the cards. When you are ready, lay out the cards in the following pattern:

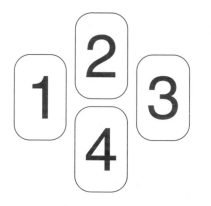

The Karmic Spread consists of four cards lain out as shown.

Katherine wanted to try this, and we thought it would be nice to show you how a Karmic Spread works. Katherine shuffled the cards, cut them, and dealt out four. Here are the cards that she got when she asked the question: *"What are the karmic lessons I'm learning now?"*

First Card: 7 of Cups. This card depicts a man trying to make a decision, but all of the choices seem to come from the world of fantasy and not reality. Which cup should he choose? Which cup would you choose? What is real and what is fantasy? These questions all figure into the interpretation of this card. The man's energy is dissipated by the fantastic visions in front of him. In this reading, the card suggests that Katherine is learning that there are many pitfalls associated with her preference for dealing with the fantasy in her head instead of the reality of the world of cash and credit and bills and invoices.

Second Card: 5 of Wands. Like all the other upright 5 cards—in numerology, 5 is the number of change—this card indicates some form of struggle. As in the previous card, the energy here is scattered, and a certain amount of confusion seems to reign. The men are striking out to defend themselves without any real sense of what the fight is about. They are confused, agitated, stressed, and fearful. Like the men in the card's image, Katherine needs to learn about what is truly threatening to her in the real world.

Third Card: 4 of Cups R. In its upright form, this card represents detachment. The young man is being offered the fourth cup, but he seems to refuse it as he is so lost in thought. Reversed, the 4 of Cups says you are coming out of your period of inaction and are ready to go in a new direction. This card indicates that Katherine is coming out of the contemplation of her fantasy and is beginning to move forward. She's learning that she is ready and able to try something new.

Fourth Card: The World. Of course, this is a wonderful card to have come up in a reading, especially in a Karmic Spread. This card indicates attainment and self-actualization. Here it suggests that Katherine has completed her present karmic lessons and can move on to the next cycle of her life. She will, of course, encounter new lessons in her next cycle. Remember that the word "now" is a key feature of this type of spread. Receiving this card tells Katherine that she has a good handle on her current life lessons and is on the path to her own abundance. Karmic rewards will follow after you accept the lessons of your past.

7 of Cups, 5 of Wands, 4 of Cups R, the World.

Now deal out four cards in your own Karmic Spread, while asking the cards *"What are the karmic lessons I am learning now?"* Before you look up the meaning of each card, spend some time studying them. In your notebook, write about what each card brings up for you.

Once you have settled on an interpretation of your Karmic Spread, think about the message the cards are sending you. Spend some time with each card, if you think they will help you to learn your present karmic lesson. One nice way to help you integrate the lesson of the cards is to draw them. Get out your art supplies again. Let your Psychic Intuition guide you and draw your own version of the card that seems the most significant to you. (Katherine is going to draw her own version of the 7 of Cups.) What you draw does not have to look the same as the actual Tarot card from your deck. Instead, allow your drawing to depict your thoughts and feelings associated with the karmic lesson the card is illuminating. Let your image be as concrete or abstract as you like. Pay attention to any flashes of insight that you may have while you are drawing. Oftentimes, when the mind is occupied in nonverbal pursuits such as drawing, your Psychic Intuition may speak up. So listen to what it has to say.

When you feel that your drawing is done, post it where you can look at it frequently. You may want to put it up on the refrigerator door, over your bed or computer, or on the bathroom mirror. Over the course of a week, see how your thoughts and feelings change about this image from your karmic lesson. If you feel so moved, try drawing another of the cards from your Karmic Spread. And be aware of any changes in your attitude. You have started your own movement through this lesson and soon will be approaching a new cycle as you travel along the path to your own abundance.

More Astrological Aspects

Now we're going to use more Astrology to look at your natural tendencies in the financial realm and to help further locate your exact fiscal position in the present day. In addition to analyzing the position of each planet in its sign and house, professional astrologers look at the relationship of the planets to each other. The planets in your chart form aspects to one another. The aspects between the financial planets in your chart can be especially significant.

Within your astrological birth chart, aspects help to describe the relationships between the planets by naming and defining the angles between the planets. The various aspects help to answer the question

"How do these planets get along?" Astrologers consider the angles of the aspects to be either favorable or challenging. Here is a list of the significant astrological aspects, their symbols, and keywords to help you understand their meaning.

Astro Aspect	Symbol	Keyword(s)
Conjunction	☌	Shares energy, focus
Sextile	⚹	Favorable
Square	□	Challenges, pushes for change
Trine	△	Eases, extremely favorable
Opposition	☍	Difficulty, extremely challenging
Quincunx	⚻	No shared energy, nothing in common

But to get a true picture of aspect and its significance, you need to get a grip on the geometry involved. Don't worry, you don't need to go dig up a protractor. You'll find the angles of Astrology's aspects easy to learn.

- **Conjunction ☌** In a conjunction, the planets sit in the same place in your chart or they are nestled closely next to each other. Conjunctions are considered to be focal points, and the interaction of the two planets involved is typically heightened and emphasized in the chart.

- **Sextile ⚹** In a sextile, the planets are 60° apart. Because the signs of each planet in a sextile share the same *yin* or *yang* energy, this is considered to be a favorable aspect.

- **Square □** In a square, the planets are 90° apart. While squares are considered to be chart challenges, they nonetheless often provide the impetus for change and improvements in your life.

- **Trine △** In a trine, the planets are 120° apart. This is the most favorable of the aspects. When planets trine each other, the signs that each planet sits in usually share the same element and the same *yin/yang* energy. For example, suppose your Jupiter ♃, which is in Virgo ♍, trines △ your Venus ♀, which is in Capricorn ♑. Virgo and Capricorn are both Earth signs and both have *yin* energy.

- **Opposition ☍** In an opposition, the planets are 180° apart. There's little in common with an opposition, but, like squares □, their difficult energy can spur you on to meet the challenges you encounter on your path.

☽ **Quincunx ⚻** In a quincunx, the planets are 150° apart. Quincunxes are interesting—nothing is shared between the two signs in which the planets sit, so some adjustment is usually required for them to interact.

Let's look at the aspects in Lisa Marie Presley's chart. The triangular grid on the bottom left is an aspect grid. This grid shows how each planet in Lisa Marie's chart relates to her other planets. To read the grid, pick a planet and follow the column or row for that planet and see which, if any, symbols show up in the boxes that represent the other planets. For example, if you start with the first column under the Moon sign ☽ and move down, you find an empty box next to the Sun ☉, Mercury ☿, and Venus ♀. This means that Lisa Marie's Moon makes no significant aspects with these three planets. Now move down to the Mars ♂ row. In the box that represents the intersection of Moon and Mars, you see the symbol for conjunction ☌. This indicates that Lisa Marie's Moon is conjunct her Mars ☽ ☌ ♂. The lines drawn through the center of her chart wheel also represent the aspects between the planets. (Note that Lisa's chart is a noon chart, so you probably will want to use the information about her Moon with some caution.)

The first things we want to focus on in Lisa Marie's chart are the conjunctions ☌ and trines △ because these are the most powerful and usually the most favorable aspects. As we pointed out earlier, Lisa Marie has her Moon conjunct her Mars ☽ ☌ ♂. This means that Lisa Marie's Mars ♂, the planet of aggression and physical energy, shares its intense energy with her Moon ☽, the planet of emotions. So Lisa Marie has intense emotions and can be highly enthusiastic.

Like many people born in the 1960s, Lisa Marie also has Pluto conjunct Uranus ♀ ☌ ♅. Pluto, the planet of power, evolution, destruction, and regeneration, shares its energy with Uranus, the planet of invention, independence, originality, and change. Because Uranus is also associated with technology and electronics, you could say that Lisa Marie's powerful need for invention and originality will be best expressed through technology and electronics. (And at the time of this writing, she was just about to release her first CD, *To Whom It May Concern,* featuring her first single, "Lights Out.")

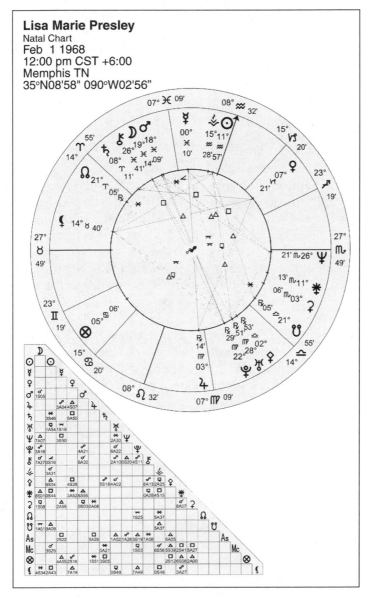

Lisa Marie Presley
Natal Chart
Feb 1 1968
12:00 pm CST +6:00
Memphis TN
35°N08'58" 090°W02'56"

Lisa Marie Presley's birth chart and aspect grid.

When we look at the trines in Lisa Marie's chart, we see Venus trine Jupiter ♀ △ ♃. Venus, the planet of love, beauty, and personal resources, is eased by Jupiter's confidence, vitality, optimism, and success. This aspect brings with it grace, elegance, a talent for making money, and the probability of many love affairs. This aspect also indicates success in the business end of the arts.

Lisa Marie also has Neptune trine the Moon $\Psi \triangle \mathtext{)}$. So Neptune, the planet of creativity, music, dreams, and illusion eases Lisa Marie's Moon, the planet of emotions. This aspect would tend to give her a lot of inborn optimism, creativity in the realm of music, and the ability to see the humor in the human condition. On the downside, this combination of planets could indicate a fuzzy focus when it comes to career or financial goals and a lack of determination.

When we look at the more challenging aspects, we find Saturn square Venus $\hbar \square \female$. So Saturn, the planet of control and limitation, challenges Lisa Marie's Venus, the planet of love, beauty, and personal resources. This alignment would tend to hinder Lisa Marie's ability to make money, and it has not helped her love life either. Luckily, her Venus is getting a boost of optimistic energy from Jupiter, as we saw above.

With Neptune square Mercury $\Psi \square \mercury$, we find that Neptune, the planet of creativity, music, dreams, and illusion, challenges Mercury, the planet of communication. This aspect might make it difficult for Lisa Marie to communicate her message in a way that people can understand.

If you keep examining Lisa Marie's chart, you will notice that she also has Jupiter opposing Mercury $\jupiter \, \delta \, \mercury$, which would tend to give her excellent communication skills, and Chiron opposing Pluto $\chiron \, \delta \, \pluto$, which is a marker for power and success in the career realm. (We talk more about Chiron $\chiron$, a planetoid only discovered in 1977, in later chapters.)

The Aspects of Your Personality

Now get out your own birth chart. Examine your aspect grid. In the space provided, note down any aspects for each of your financial planets. If your Venus is conjunct your Mercury (and Katherine's is), you would write $\female \, \sigma \, \mercury$.

Venus ♀	Mars ♂	Jupiter ♃	Saturn ♄
_____	_____	_____	_____
_____	_____	_____	_____
_____	_____	_____	_____

To bring home the meaning of the aspect pairs you have noted, try writing a sentence for each one. For example, take $\female \, \sigma \, \mercury$, and you get Venus, the planet of love, beauty, and personal resources, shares energy with Mercury, the planet of communication. This pairing could indicate a love of writing and an ability to make money or enhance one's personal resources through writing and communications. Look at Appendix A if you need to for quick reference to the energies of the planets.

Now you know more about how the planets are impacting on your financial situation. Remember that Astrology describes your natural tendencies. It does not write your fate in stone. No one is doomed to be broke all the time. If you have challenging aspects in your chart, you can work to overcome them and move toward the kind of life and relationship to money that you envision for yourself. Note, too, that the favorable aspects—trines and conjunctions—are more powerful than the unfavorable ones. So the likelihood is that the planets and their energies are helping you and not holding you back.

Once you understand the astrological energies that have helped to shape you, your personality, psychology, and the ways you handle money, you can focus on changing them. If you want to! Or you can learn to use all of what you have—your good habits as well as your bad ones—to help match your financial style to your own image of yourself so you can get more of what you want from life.

Money and Abundance in Relationship

Arguing over money is one of the major divisive factors that comes between people in relationships. Sometimes one person in a couple acts like the sneaky man in the 7 of Swords. Sometimes one half of a pair is super responsible, precise, and in control with regard to money matters (think 4 of Pentacles) and the other half is indifferent (like the 4 of Cups) or careless. You can use Astrology to find out how closely your natural tendencies with money match your life partner's money style.

What's your money style?

By using Astrology's synastry grid, you can compare your two birth charts. The grid will show the relationship of each planet in your chart to the planets in your partner's. The planets in your chart form aspects to the planets in your partner's chart, just the way they do within your own chart. These aspects are a significant indication of the type of relationship that you have and of the kind of energy (and resources) you share.

Because you are already familiar with Lisa Marie Presley's chart, let's look at the synastry grid that represents her birth chart as it lines up with her ex-husband Michael Jackson.

Across
Michael Jackson
Natal Chart
Aug 29 1958
12:00 pm CDT +5:00
Gary IN
41°N35'36" 087°W20'47"

Down
Lisa Marie Presley
Natal Chart
Feb 1 1968
12:00 pm CST +6:00
Memphis TN
35°N08'58" 090°W02'56"

	☽	☉	☿	♀	♂	♃	♄	♅	♆	♇	⚷	⚸	♀	✷	?	☊	☋	As	Mc	⊗	☽
☽			2S33	2A40		0S06		1S40			1S49					3S14	3A53	6S14	3A28	1S00	
☉				4A44		1A32			7A22							4A03		1A03		6A17	
☿	5A40	4S37				1S41			2A24	1A59	2A14	5S14	6A20			7S03					
♀	3A43	1S31				0S28				5S12			0S51					5A39	0A20		
♂	7S05		1S28	3A45		0A58		0S35			0S44			2S09				5S09		0A05	
♃	2S36	7A41				4A45			0A40	1A05	0A50	8A17	3S16								
♄	2S21	2A22		1S17			5A18					1A46						0S29			
♅				6A57		0A22											0A51				
♆		0S47		4S27					5A49			1S24							3S39		
♇				0A36		3A22					5A05		6A30		0S38			4A15	1A18		
⚷		1S07			1A48	1A48								1A19							
⚸			1A13		3A39	1S59			3A51	1A56			0A32	7A39		2S28	7A13	2A46	5A44		
♀			1A12						1S26											0S21	
✷	0S09	5S23	5A28		2A16					6A12			4A47					1A47		7A01	
?	7A58	2A44			4S37	1A01		0S32	0S56				3A25								
☊	0A15	4S29	4A24		1A58	7A36			1A46	3A40	3S52		0S26		2S02	2S02		1S37		0S07	
☋	0A15		4A24	0S49	1A58				1A46	3A40			0S26		2S02	2S02		1S37		0S07	
As		2A15			5A55	0A40			4A21				2A52					5A07			
Mc	2A42							4A57	5A58							2A02			4A28		
⊗	5A59	0A45			1A48	6A36			2A31	2A56	0A46				1A25			7A55		1A51	
☽	3S36	8S50		2A01	7A14			1S11			4A39	2A45			1A20			1S40		3A34	

For Lisa Marie Presley's planets, read down. For Michael Jackson's planets, read across.

The planets' symbols on the left side of the figure and reading down are Lisa Marie's. The planets across the top of the chart represent the heavenly bodies in Michael Jackson's birth chart. You read the chart just the way you read the aspect chart earlier in this chapter. For example, start with Michael's Sun ☉, which is the second symbol on the top of the chart. Move down the column underneath the ☉ symbol. The first two boxes, which represent Lisa's Moon ☽ and Sun ☉, are empty. This means that Michael's Sun does not form any significant aspects with these two planets in Lisa's chart. Move down one more box to Lisa's Mercury ☿ and you will see the opposition sign ☍. Michael's Sun is in opposition to Lisa's Mercury. So Michael's Sun, the planet of the self, causes difficulty with the energy of Lisa's Mercury, the planet of communications. This alignment would tend to hinder communications between the two. But let's focus on the financial planets and see what we can learn about the money issues that came up between Lisa Marie and Michael.

Venus ♀. Lisa Marie's Venus trines Michael's Sun ♀ △ ☉. Because the Sun in a person's birth chart can represent the person him- or herself, we can say that Michael himself eases Lisa's Venus, the planet of love, beauty, and personal resources. As you can imagine, this aspect between the two charts would cause Lisa to feel very attracted to Michael. So much so that while they were together ideas of business probably didn't even enter her head.

Lisa Marie's Venus also trines Michael's Pluto ♀ △ ♇. In other words, Michael's Pluto, the planet of power, evolution, destruction, and regeneration, eases Lisa Marie's Venus, the planet of love, beauty, and personal resources. All of Michael's Pluto power connected to Lisa's personal resources would have made these two super-successful business partners. This alignment between their two planets could also indicate a strong sexual attraction.

Michael's Venus is opposing Lisa Marie's Sun ♀ ☍ ☉. Lisa Marie's Sun (and Lisa Marie herself) causes difficulty with the energy of Michael's planet of love, beauty, and personal resources. This conjunction could cause mutual dislike between the two parties, and it probably did not help Michael with his business dealings.

Mars ♂. Lisa Marie's Mars squares Michael's Saturn ♂ □ ♄. Here the two planets are challenging each other, and it looks nasty. This combination makes for intolerance in love and in business.

Michael's Mars trines Lisa Marie's Uranus and her Pluto ♂ △ ♅ ♇ and opposes her Neptune ♂ ☍ ♆. This combination of planets between the two charts indicates yet more sexual connection. Business and money matters in their union were the furthest motivation from their minds!

Jupiter ♃. Lisa Marie's Jupiter is conjunct Michael's Sun and his Mercury ♃ ☌ ☉ ☿, and Michael's Jupiter trines Lisa Marie's Mercury ♃ △ ☿, which would tend to indicate that the two share great understanding and kindness and can really help each other out. In addition, Lisa Marie's Jupiter conjuncts Michael's Pluto ♃ ☌ ♇. So her planet of confidence, vitality, optimism, and success shares energy with Michael's planet of power, evolution, destruction, and regeneration. This combination would tend to indicate that the two people involved share ideas about careers, success, ambition, and abundance, and they are able to work well together toward their common goals.

Saturn ♄. Lisa Marie's Saturn trines Michael's Uranus ♄ △ ♅. Lisa Marie's planet of control and limitation impacts Michael's planet of invention, independence, originality, and change. This could indicate a desire on Lisa Marie's part to control Michael—his creativity and source of livelihood—and a wish to change him in these areas.

Michael's Saturn squares Lisa Marie's Moon and her Pluto ♄ □ ☽ ♇. Here Michael's planet of control and limitation is impacting on Lisa Marie's planet of emotions (the Moon) and her planet of power, evolution, destruction, and regeneration. With these aspects, we see Michael's desire to control Lisa Marie and her power, which to a large extent in Lisa Marie's case is tied to her inherited wealth.

Just from examining the aspects formed by the four financial planets, we can see that Lisa Marie and Michael had a very complex relationship. The synastry grid between them shows some very hard challenges in regards to money, values, prosperity, and how to handle the financial aspects of a marriage. The fact that Michael developed his wealth over a period of time and that Lisa Marie had inherited wealth that was established early in her life is also a factor here, because, of course, differences in how one attained wealth can be a point of challenge and adjustment. As Arlene put it, "It will be hard for this relationship to endure the differing points of view on money and prosperity. In other words, their differing values will create dysfunctional handling of money causing some inevitable outcomes." And of course, we know that these two split up.

Knowing what your natural tendencies are with relation to your partner and to the control of funds can help you both to get along. If you know that you have a tendency to try to control your partner's spending, you can either work to curb that habit or you can make arrangements with your partner so that that behavior on your part is not bothersome or restrictive.

Because we know that you're curious, here's a peek at Michael Jackson's birth chart. Notice that the chart has a great many aspects, all of which are indicative of aspects of Michael's unique talents. (Also note that Michael's, like Lisa Marie's, is a noon chart.)

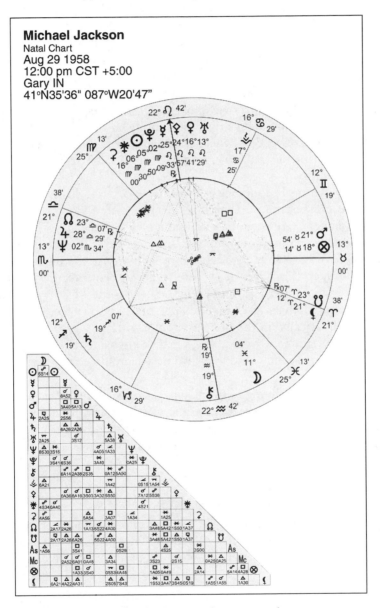

Michael Jackson's birth chart and aspect grid.

In terms of Michael's finances, we were interested to note that he has Venus trine Saturn ♀ △ ♄. So Michael's planet of control and limitation impacts his planet of love, beauty, and personal resources. This aspect would tend to give Michael a great deal of control over his finances. He is also ambitious in the financial realm and quite able to accumulate resources.

Michael's Saturn also trines his Uranus ♄ △ ♅. In this case, Michael's planet of control and limitation impacts his planet of invention, independence, originality, and change. Keeping in mind that Uranus is also associated with technology and electronics, it comes as no surprise that Michael has been able to command attention through mass media and to move his fans emotionally through the use of that technology. The downside of this aspect, though, is the tendency to hold extremely unconventional ideas, especially with regard to societal rules and morality.

Michael's Venus is conjunct his Uranus ♀ ♂ ♅. So his planet of love, beauty, and personal resources shares energy with his planet of invention, independence, originality, and change. This aspect is what has allowed Michael to be such a unique, innovative, and often eccentric artist. Here his Astrology says he will be able to use the media to be revolutionary, cutting edge, or even outrageous. This aspect also indicates a love of change. The desire for the new could be part of what has influenced Michael to change his personal appearance (or his beauty) so drastically. In the business realm, this aspect could be helpful in the entertainment world, but, on the downside, could lead Michael into a perpetual resource-draining search for the new and the exciting.

Of course, there are many more aspects to Michael's unique personality. If you feel so inclined, use the analysis here as a jumping-off point and spend some more time learning about this member of pop's royal family. Or move on, and study your own aspects—both personal and interpersonal.

Your Synastry and Your Assets

If you already have a synastry grid for you and your partner, take it out now. If you don't have one, you can have a professional astrologer draw one for you. In Appendix A, we provide information about where to get such work done.

Before you start with the serious analysis, get an overall sense of how you get along astrologically. Start by looking over your grid for the favorable aspects—conjunctions ☌ and trines △. Then look for your chart challenges—the squares □ and oppositions ☍. Now, examine your financial planets one by one and note which aspects they make to the planets in your partner's chart.

Venus ♀	Mars ♂	Jupiter ♃	Saturn ♄

Once you have the list of your and your partner's combined planetary aspects in the financial realm, spend some time meditating on your list. You may want to make sentences for each aspect pair the way that we did for Lisa Marie and Michael Jackson. Remember that the beneficial aspects—trines and conjunctions—are stronger than the challenging ones. Keep in mind, too, that despite anything that your astrological chart has to say, you always have free will. Allow your knowledge of Astrology and the insight that it has given you into your finances and your relationship to help you achieve your financial goals and move closer to your own personal abundance.

chapter 6

Bankrupt, Flat-Out Broke, Negative Assets, and Other Defaults

Saturn returns and your credit
Progress in your astrological birth chart
The punch of Pluto
Down, but not out: More Pluto transits
Tarot's Pentacles reveal the ebb and flow of abundance
Your Psychic Intuition leads to action

Perhaps you feel yourself drowning in debt. Your credit card bills keep growing, and with each passing day, you see more and more of your abundance slip down the drain. What do you do when your balance sheet shows that you're in the red? In this chapter, we explore how financial issues can be connected to planetary cycles, such as Saturn returns, which happen about every 30 years, and the demanding transits of distant and slow-moving Pluto. We show you how you can learn to work with your planetary cycles instead of against them, and we take a journey through Tarot's Minor Arcana Pentacles to see how the images on these cards mirror the natural ebb and flow of your abundance. Finally, we provide an exercise to help you work through your problems with the aid of your Psychic Intuition. Working toward a more prosperous future will take effort—but using the tools of Astrology, Tarot, and Psychic Intuition can make this work fun.

Down and Out?

By late 2002, consumer credit card spending was up 8.1 percent over previous quarters and home mortgage foreclosures and filings for personal bankruptcy had reached new all-time highs. The average U.S. credit card holder owes more than $4,000 on plastic alone! We are not telling you this to scare you. We want you to know that many people carry a lot of debt. We want to assure you that if you are broke and in debt and anxious, you are not alone. We are a nation of overspenders. Even the most prosperous among us have periods of financial concern, worry, anxiety, and frustration. The periodic demands of Saturn ♄ returns and the impact of Pluto ♀ transits are just a few of the astrological cycles that can impact your finances by throwing you out of balance and maybe even pushing you into overspending and debt. One of the keys to a successful relationship with money is an understanding of the timing these types of occurrences, whether in one's own astrological birth chart or because of planetary cycles. Learning how to work with both your own and more global planetary rhythms could help you navigate away from failure and debt and toward the abundance and security that you crave.

Caveat Emptor

Let the buyer beware! More specifically, let the buyer who pays with a credit card beware. We know you know this, but we think it bears repeating: That bargain you picked up yesterday on sale is no bargain if you pay with a credit card and carry a balance on your card. Credit card companies are in the business of making money, and they make money off of you every time you let your full balance go unpaid and allow them to hit you with finance charges. Credit cards are big business for the companies that issue them. For example, about 25 million people in the United States have active Sears accounts. This end of the business is such a moneymaker that, at the time of this writing, Sears had five major companies bidding to buy its credit card portfolio. In fact, the credit card fees on Sears cards make up 60 percent of the company's profits. That's money that Sears shoppers (and perhaps this group includes you) could have kept and saved.

You can guard against credit card debt by being a sensible shopper. And you can use Astrology to help you stay sensible. There will be times in all of our lives when we are more prone to bad judgment, overspending, and financial losses. In Chapter 4, we looked at the influence that the cycles of the Moon ☽ can have on your finances and business dealings. Here we take a look at the cycles of Saturn ♄ and Pluto ♇, two heavy hitters that can pack a wallop to your wallet and your bank account.

Saturn ♄ takes 29½ years to complete one orbit around the Sun. So your Saturn return occurs at about age 29½, when Saturn returns to the place in the sky where it was at the date and time of your birth. Because Saturn moves fairly slowly, you will probably feel the impact of its approach to your natal Saturn for some time. Katherine is convinced that she felt the influence of her Saturn return for three years. When Arlene had her Saturn return between the ages of 29 and 30, she started her new career in metaphysics, and left the restaurant industry where she had worked for 10 years. During her Saturn return, Arlene felt like something in her life was fading away; as much as she had loved all her jobs in the restaurant business, during this period she was just plain disinterested. Saturn returns bring change and often some form of loss. If you try to hold on to something that you need to let go of, your Saturn return may very well shake you enough to make sure that you do let go.

Your Saturn return may include the following:

- ☯ Acknowledgment that certain things have lost importance in your life, including dreams or goals that you now realize no longer matter to you.

- ☯ A new commitment to an exciting undertaking, such as a new career, a major change that will affect you for years to come. "I'm not getting any younger," you may think. "I'd better (fill in the blank) before it's too late." Your Saturn return will bring out your serious side (Saturn's a super-sober planet), so you will approach this change with caution and care.

- ☯ After a few years of feeling responsible and grown up, you'll start having fun again. A Saturn return does force you to let go of the old, but it also helps you build a firm new foundation. Once that foundation is in place, you'll be able to relax and enjoy again.

Let's look at an example of a Saturn return and its impact on one young woman's life and her finances.

Save Me

You may have heard of Karyn. Karyn lives in New York City, and although she had a good job, she also had hefty credit card debts. As of this writing, Karyn has paid off her debts, and she did so in an unusual way. But she started off the way many people do. In August 2001, when she realized that her debt was out of control—at one point, she owed as much as $25,000 on credit cards—she contacted a credit-counseling agency. A few months later, in an effort to cut her expenses, she moved to a cheaper apartment in Brooklyn. At that point, her debt was at an all-time high, and, as she put it, "I started freaking out about it the most." On June 21, 2002, she posted a message to Craig's List, a website that runs free classified ads, asking for help. Then, on June 23, 2002, she created a website for herself—www.savekaryn.com—where she solicited donations. People responded to her pleas. Karyn raised more than $13,000 with her site.

Let's take a look at Karyn's astrological birth chart and her transits.

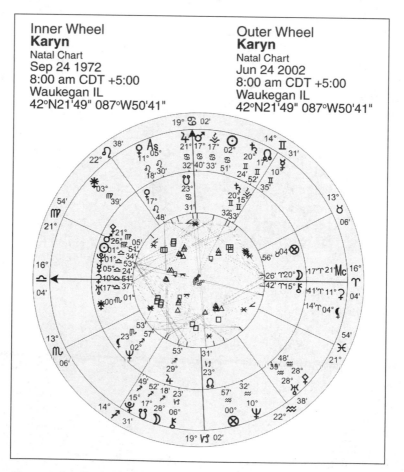

Karyn's birth chart appears on the inside wheel. The outside wheel represents the planets in the sky on June 24, 2002.

The illustration shows Karyn's birth chart in the center with her transits for June 24, 2002, on the outside wheel. This is one easy way to see where the planets are in the sky for a given day and how they relate to your natal chart.

On the inner wheel, find Karyn's Saturn ♄ in her 9th house in Gemini ♊. Now look on the outer wheel. Notice that Saturn in the sky is also in Gemini and is in almost the exact same position as Karyn's natal Saturn. So Karyn experienced her Saturn return at this time of significant financial events in her life. And Saturn did make her change her ways!

We think Karyn's story is instructive. Whatever your opinion of her method, Karyn, coupled with her Saturn return, changed and eventually took control of her debt. If you are faced with what looks like insurmountable debt, you can act, take control, and banish debt from your life, too—even if you've already had your first Saturn return and aren't due for another one for a good many years. To find a credit-counseling agency near you, call the National Foundation for Credit Counseling at 1-800-388-2227. This number connects you to a 24-hour automated list of approved credit-counseling offices. Or visit their website at www.debtadvice.org for listings and lots of educational resources that can help you manage your debt. You may also want to check out Karyn's website and read more about her journey from debt-ridden to debt-free.

If you know that you are due for a Saturn return, you may want to check your birth chart and find out from an astrological calendar where Saturn ♄ is in the sky. Or consult a professional astrologer. Then brace yourself, and watch your wallet. A little caution in the spending arena could serve you well during a Saturn return, and you will come through your Saturn return a little older and quite a bit wiser.

Another type of chart that professional astrologers like Arlene may draw up for you once you have reached the age when Saturn returns become a concern is a progressed chart. A progressed chart shows how you have grown and matured. To "progress" a chart, the astrologer plots the planets a day forward in time for every year you have been alive. So if you are 30 years old this year, your astrologer progresses your chart by 30 days to see how time has changed you. Here is Karyn's progressed chart.

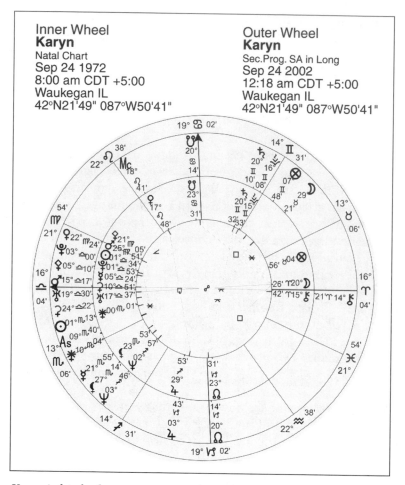

Inner Wheel
Karyn
Natal Chart
Sep 24 1972
8:00 am CDT +5:00
Waukegan IL
42°N21'49" 087°W50'41"

Outer Wheel
Karyn
Sec.Prog. SA in Long
Sep 24 2002
12:18 am CDT +5:00
Waukegan IL
42°N21'49" 087°W50'41"

Karyn's birth chart appears on the inside wheel. The outside wheel is her progressed chart, which represents how she has grown and matured.

The inner wheel is Karyn's birth chart, and the outer wheel is her progressed chart. Notice that Saturn ♄ is in pretty much the same place in both charts. This, of course, is because Karyn is still so young, and Saturn is a slow-moving planet. If you look at the faster-moving planets, you will see more change. Mercury ☿ in Karyn's birth chart is in her 12th house in Libra ♎. In her progressed chart, Mercury is in her 2nd house in Scorpio ♏. You will find Karyn's natal Venus ♀ in her 10th house in Leo ♌. In her progressed chart, Venus appears in her 12th house in the sign of Virgo ♍. One thing that an astrologer looks for in a progressed chart is new aspects created between the planets. These aspects can show emerging skills or future challenges.

The new aspects beginning to form within a progressed chart will challenge you to learn new ways of handling the issues in your life. At first, you may feel uncomfortable or just differently about your life and your situation. Usually you feel this shift and have a sense that no specific event relates to your new feelings. After a few months, you may notice that your attitude toward a given subject has totally changed. For example, when your progressed Venus ♀ starts to aspect the planets in your natal chart, you will notice a positive flow of energy or an upbeat attitude toward the areas that the aspected planets represent. Venus can bring a "love" of that situation. All of a sudden you may develop a passion for going to the ballet, whereas before you just weren't very interested or excited by dance. (Progressed Venus ♀ aspecting your natal Mars ♂ might bring you just such a new enthusiasm.) In the previous chart, Karyn's progressed Venus ♀ is approaching her Sun ☉. This could indicate a growing self-love, which probably aided Karyn in finding a new approach to her debt problem.

The Power of Pluto ♀

Pluto, the slowest-moving planet in our solar system, takes 248 years to complete one orbit of the Sun. Because it moves so slowly, Pluto ♀ can stay in one sign for up to 32 years. As a result, most people born in the same generation have Pluto in the same sign. Pluto is the planet of transformation, and like the Roman god for whom it is named, it is also associated with death and the underworld. Pluto is also associated with the atom and with nuclear energy. So you'd be right to say that Pluto is one intense planet!

You will probably feel every planetary transit that affects your chart to some extent. With Pluto you will know for sure that something major is happening to you because nothing hits like a Pluto ♀ transit. When Pluto comes around to square your natal Pluto, ♀ □ ♀, which will be sometime between ages 36 and 45 for most of you reading this book, you will pay attention, because it's midlife crisis time. (If you were born in the 1930s, though, because of the planet's irregular orbit, your Pluto transit hits you later—around the time of your forty-ninth birthday.) This type of Pluto transit lasts about two years. During this time, you may find yourself acting uncharacteristically. You may, for example, all of a sudden run out and spend too much money on a sleek new sports car. If you're reading this before you have experienced your own Pluto square Pluto transit, be forewarned and watch yourself. If you have already been through your Pluto square Pluto, keep your eyes opened for some of the other major hits that Pluto can inflict.

Pluto's transit over what are known as the four angles of your chart—your ascendant, midheaven, descendent, and IC (the cusp of your 4th house)—mark true turning points in your life. For example, Pluto transiting over your ascendant, which is also your 1st house cusp, always makes for major change and forced transformation. Sometimes the experience is not unpleasant, but most of the time this type of transit is a total challenge for the individual involved. This type of Pluto transit can change your attitude toward all the issues with which the 1st house concerns itself—your self, your identity, your appearance, and your instincts. With all of the four angles, Pluto can make for long-term change in your life and lifestyle. It will also affect your attitudes with regard to the issues of the houses associated with each angle. Because Pluto moves so slowly, most people will only experience Pluto transits over two of the four angles of their birth chart.

Here's a little table that outlines how a Pluto transit over the angles of your chart can transform you. Notice that an angle to your ascendant, because it will impact your body, mind, and emotional self, will cause the most profound and broad-reaching changes in your life.

Angle	Chart Location	Life Area Affected
Ascendant	Cusp of the 1st house	The self
Nadir	Cusp of the 4th house	Family
Descendant	Cusp of the 7th house	Relationships
Midheaven	Cusp of the 10th house	Career

If Pluto transits over your natal Sun ☉ and Moon ☽, you will experience another type of transformation and rebirth. When Pluto ♀ opposes ☍ (causes difficulty with) or squares □ (challenges) a planet in your birth chart, there will be huge movement in your personal life. To relieve the uneasy tension created by these two aspects, you will probably have to change: Pluto says leave that old idea, concept, or attitude behind—or else! Of course, if you are broke, this could be great news. Pluto is going to see to it that you leave your approach to money behind, and you can be reborn as a fiscally solvent person. Arlene likes to describe the power or energy when Pluto makes an opposition or a square like this: Suppose you leave a pot of water boiling until all the water boils away. Then you realize your pot is burning. It's too hot to handle, but you have to grab it and get it off the flame before the metal becomes hot enough to start a fire. Yow!

Under a Pluto transit, you may experience loss, but you will also come to truly understand that you can survive these losses. You will learn that something will always replace what you have lost. The lesson of Pluto is to accept the change/death and rebirth of your situation. You will never be left in a void.

Who'll Buy My Memories?

You looked at Willie Nelson's chart in Chapter 3, and we're going to take a look at his stars again. This time we've given you a transit chart. On the inside of the wheel, you will find Nelson's birth chart. The outside wheel shows the planets in the sky for November 1990, which was when the IRS came to his home in Texas and confiscated all of his property because of the amount of money he owed them.

You can see from all the aspect lines drawn through the center of this chart that there is a lot going on here. You might want to take a quick look at Nelson's birth chart just for comparison's sake.

One of the interesting things about Willie Nelson's transit chart is that Pluto (the planet of transformation) was in Scorpio ♀ ♏ in his 4th house and very close to the IC (4th house cusp). You'll remember that the 4th house concerns itself with issues of home, family, and your roots. At the same time, Saturn ♄, which can signal loss or restriction, was in Capricorn ♑ in his 6th house of work and job issues.

In addition, Pluto ♀ squares the ascendant of his chart. We saw that Pluto sits in Scorpio ♏, and Willie's ascendant is Leo ♌. Further-more, if you look down at the bottom of the transit chart, you will see a whole group of planets lined up in Scorpio ♏. Notice that they are in opposition ☍ to his Sun ☉ and to his Venus ♀ and thus are causing difficulty with the energy of both of those important planets. The challenge to his Sun ☉ can be seen as a challenge to Nelson himself and to his vitality. The challenge to Venus ♀ is an attack on the love, beauty, and personal resources in Nelson's life. You can tell from all this planetary activity in the sky that something major was going to happen to Willie Nelson and to his sense of abundance. But we're not done. In addition to all of this, the transiting Moon ☽ was in Aries ♈ in Nelson's 9th house, the house of legal issues, and at the same time, the transiting Moon was conjunct Nelson's natal Uranus ☽ ☌ ♅, the planet that can signal sudden change.

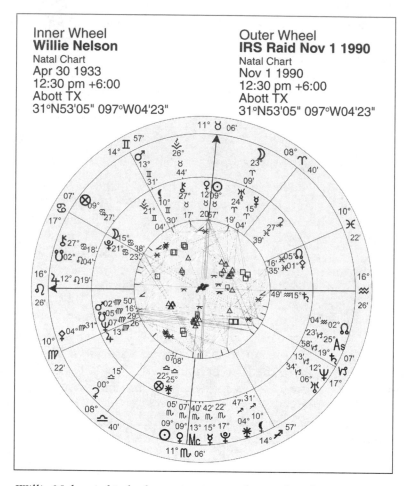

Willie Nelson's birth chart appears on the inside wheel. The out-side wheel shows his transits during the time of his IRS raid.

Willie Nelson's story with the IRS does have a happy ending. Even though they took all of his possessions, including his gold records and mementos such as bronzed baby shoes, Nelson was able to bounce back. He made a deal; he cut an album, called *Who'll Buy My Memories: The IRS Tapes,* all of the profits of which went directly to the IRS to cover what he owed. Willie Nelson cleared his debt in 1993, and that same year was elected to the Country Music Hall of Fame.

You may want to order a transit chart from a professional astrologer and check out the relationship between your natal Pluto and Pluto in the sky. If you are prepared for your Pluto transits, you can use their tranformative power to help you move along the path toward your abundance.

Tarot's Pentacles: The Ebb and Flow of Your Assets

What goes up must come down. Or in this case, what is down—the level of your funds—must come up. Just like the tides or the seasons of the year, our assets have a natural ebb and flow. Sometimes even the most affluent individual has financial issues—whether it be a cash-flow problem, a negative change in investment value, or the loss of income due to corporate layoffs. Take a lesson from Pluto ♀ and know that something will always replace what you have lost. Winter and the feelings of cold barrenness will end, and like Persephone you will emerge from the underworld. Flowers will bloom, birds will sing, and it will be spring once again.

One good way to explore the cycles of your abundance is to take a journey through Tarot's Pentacles. Pentacles are the cards of the financial and material world. By traveling through these 10 cards, you can look at your relationship to your assets—their highs, lows, and in-between states. Grab your Tarot deck and pull out the Ace through 10 of Pentacles. Place them in a row, from lowest to highest, in front of you.

Once you have the Pentacles all laid out, you can get the full sweep of what the cards depict. No matter which style of Tarot deck you prefer, security, pride, and work are evident in all the images. The Ace of Pentacles is the beginning of a new business or a newfound sense of wealth. As you move through the 2, 3, and 4 of Pentacles, you can see prosperity growing. As in any natural process, setbacks occur; but by the time you reach the 8, 9, and 10 of Pentacles, you see images of stability, security, financial well-being, and independence. The higher the number on the card, the more secure and abundant you will have become. Let's look at these 10 cards one by one to see what they can tell us about the natural ebb and flow of personal finance.

*The Ace of Pentacles res-
onates to the number 1, the
number of new beginnings.*

The Ace of Pentacles can describe the start of a new business or the beginning of prosperity or wealth. Just as the cloud-encircled hand offers you a shiny pentacle coin, this card can signal a gift, an inheritance, or a valuable award. This card often comes up to tell you that you are developing a good financial foundation or a supportive home environment and thus, by following your good common sense, are on the road to your own future abundance.

When the Ace of Pentacles is reversed, however, the card describes loss, lack, frustration, and delays. You may have headed down the wrong road and as a result will have to hold tight to your assets. When this card comes up in a reading, you'd be advised to take a close look at your bank balance. You also will want to guard against feelings of greed. Perhaps money and material goods are less important to your overall well-being and ultimate prosperity than matters of the heart and spirit.

*The 2 of Pentacles res-
onates to the number 2, the
number of balance.*

The juggler in the 2 of Pentacles has it all in balance. Sure, he has to work to maintain the balance, but he knows that he can handle his situation, and he takes a certain joy in the activity. When this card comes up for you, know that you have the ability to handle what life is throwing your way. You can juggle the opportunities, possibilities, and decisions that come before you with confidence. You may have to exert yourself, but you will be able to use your strength and stamina to persevere and maintain harmony and balance.

With the 2 of Pentacles R, the juggler seems to have lost his balance and with it his sense of joy, accomplishment, and harmony. This card can herald a difficult decision or discouraging news that may cause a setback in your plans and projects. The card can also tell you that lack of organization or overcommitment is holding you back; you need to let something go. You may be spending too much money on unnecessary or frivolous things.

The 3 of Pentacles resonates to the number 3, the number of creativity.

Congratulations! In its upright position, the 3 of Pentacles acknowledges that you have learned new skills or information. Like the stonemason in the picture, you will gain approval for your creativity and work talents. This approval may lead to monetary gain in the form of a raise. Or you may be granted an award, an honor, or membership in a professional organization or club.

When this card is reversed, the reality of your situation does not match your ideal or plan. You may be suffering from a lack of passion in your work, and as a result what you produce is sloppy. You may not have the tools or the information that you need to get the job done, and labor problems or unsafe conditions may hinder your progress.

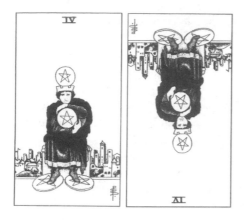

The 4 of Pentacles resonates to the number 4, the number of security.

In the 4 of Pentacles, the central figure is holding tightly to what he has. He's worked hard for his security. This card can indicate a certain conservative approach to your funds. It can also say that you are acting the role of the miser. You have demonstrated good judgment with your money and have a firm financial foundation. You may enjoy life more if you loosen your grip just a tad.

Reversed, the 4 of Pentacles says that you may be spending more than you actually have or more than you had planned to spend. If this card comes up for you in this position, better balance that checkbook right away and use caution when spending. Be careful, too, not to lose money accidentally. You may be behaving very generously—too generously, in fact, for the size of your bank account.

The 5 of Pentacles resonates to the number 5, the number of change.

Here fortune is at a low ebb. The 5 of Pentacles can describe a deep personal loss. The loss can be purely financial—loss of a job, or money. Or the card can indicate a more spiritual condition—a feeling of separation or alienation from one's workplace, family, friends, or community. This card sometimes comes up when you have neglected your body or spirit due to overwork or a tendency toward workaholic behaviors. In this case, the card tells you it's time for a change.

In its reversed position, this card is much more positive, indicating renewed hope and optimism after loss. Your negative cycle and bad luck have come to an end. Your courage has returned, and with it you have gained a greater understanding of the ebb and flow of all matter and energy in our lives. You are now in a position to reap what you have sown.

The 6 of Pentacles resonates to the number 6, the number of responsibility.

The 6 of Pentacles shows a man sharing his wealth with others or distributing a bonus. When this card comes up for you, it may indicate that extra monetary help will be offered to you. This could take the form of a bonus, a gift, or an inheritance. Financial reward and a possible new job are yours. This card can also say that you are now in a position to share what you have with others. Either way, this is good news! Remember that your giving will often pave the way to you receiving more of what you want and need.

The 6 of Pentacles R advises you to be cautious of what others offer you. The gift you are being given may come with strings attached. If you are expecting a bonus at work or a piece of someone's estate, it may turn out to be smaller than what you had anticipated.

You may be in a situation in which your investments are losing value or your prosperity is threatened because your contributions and hard work are not getting their due. In the reversed position, this card can also warn you about underhanded business practices, which may involve deception or bribery.

The 7 of Pentacles resonates to the number 7, the number of inner wisdom.

The farmer in the 7 of Pentacles brims with self-confidence. He knows that he has worked hard and will receive payment for his skills. When this card comes up, it could be telling you that your investments will bring a good return. Like the farmer's, your hard work and planning will pay off. While this card does not say that you will be wealthy, it does indicate a comfortable financial independence.

In its reversed position, the 7 of Pentacles shows the farmer's pentacles falling away from him. This card can indicate poor speculation—gambling and losing on what you thought was a sure thing. Your investment may show no profit, or your crops could fail due to bad weather. In this position this card can also indicate problems with land or real estate. If you get this card in a reading, you would do well to be cautious when spending.

The 8 of Pentacles resonates to the number 8, the number of achievement.

The craftsman in the 8 of Pentacles is totally focused on his own productivity. He is hardworking, skillful, and quick. This card recognizes a job well done and the profit and recognition that come with that facility. The card also indicates that you will further develop your skills and your ability to profit by them. Through your hard work, you will not only get better at what you do, but will gain social approval as well.

When the 8 of Pentacles is reversed, the craftsman is no longer productive. This can indicate delays in a work project due to workplace problems or sloppy and inferior work. The poor work, in turn, will lead to poor profits. Lack of balance in your personal life may be contributing to your poor performance at work. You may be suffering from job burnout, in which case it may be time to start looking for a new career.

The 9 of Pentacles resonates to the number 9, the number of transformation.

The 9 of Pentacles represents all the comforts of the home and the garden. The woman depicted here is well dressed, calm, secure, and surrounded by riches. She is strongly connected to her harmonious environment. This card speaks of self-sufficiency and independence. If you get this card in a reading, you will know that you are on the true road to prosperity. In fact, you will have so much bounty that you will be able to share your wealth with others.

In its reversed position, the 9 of Pentacles describes an image of financial insecurity. Upside down, the woman is no longer secure or serene. When this card comes up for you, your very foundations have been shaken, and as a result you are not comfortable in your own home. Your future and your investments look uncertain, and you are probably dealing with a great deal of fear and anxiety about your financial situation.

The 10 of Pentacles resonates back to the number 1, the number of new beginnings—and a secure and stable home.

Success is yours! The 10 of Pentacles represents the height of financial security. In this card, the entire family has worked to secure the future of all its members. In a reading, this card will often come up when you are in a position to buy a house or a car. Your investments will see you through and support you in your maturity and your old age. Even your grandchildren will benefit from the stable foundation that you have built.

In the reversed position, this card shows the family engaged in a feud. The fight is probably over money or stock, and it could very well ruin any financial stability that has been achieved. The wealth of the entire family is at risk. If this card comes up for you in a reading, be cautious with investments. A weak economy or poor management could reduce your assets.

Pick Your Pentacle

Allow your Psychic Intuition to guide you and pick one of the Pentacle cards described above. Pick whichever card you feel most strongly draws you. You may know why you picked the card. You may feel that the card represents the situation you are in now, or that the card you've selected represents what you want. But you don't have to know why the card you've picked has attracted you.

Spend some time examining the card, and then take out your notebook. Open to a clean sheet of paper and quickly write a list of five things that you like about your card.

Read your list over and know that all of the good things that you saw in your card are also inside you. You may need to do some work, or some letting go, to allow these good qualities to manifest, but they are there inside you.

Turn to another sheet of paper. Keep the card in front of you and list five positive things that the people or figures on your card would do if they were in your financial situation.

Now read your second list. Pick one action from this list, circle it on the page, and commit to doing it. Give yourself a time frame for when you should have your action completed. Write the date for the completion of your action in your notebook, too.

Third Chakra Pentacle Meditation

To help you execute your Pentacle action plan, try this short third chakra meditation. The chakras are energy centers in the body that lie along your spine. Each of the seven chakras regulates a different energy in the body. You can think of them as swirling balls of light. Your third chakra, which is located at your solar plexus, governs your will and is associated with the color yellow. Third chakra meditations can help to balance your energy, facilitate decision-making, and aid you in developing and sticking to a plan of action.

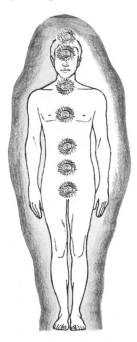

Chakras are energy centers in the body. The third chakra is located at your solar plexus.

Stand in yoga's mountain pose, sit on the floor in an easy meditation pose or in a chair, or lie down on a hard surface. Straighten your spine. Place your hands over your solar plexus and continue to breathe. If you like, hold the Pentacle card that you picked against your solar plexus, too. Close your eyes and focus on your breathing.

Imagine the Pentacle you picked. In your mind's eye, focus on the pentacles (or pentacle, if you picked the Ace) on your card. See their bright shade of yellow. Imagine that they are shining in the sunlight. Allow the color to fill you up. Feel the swirling yellow energy inside you. With each exhale, allow worry and distracting thoughts to leave your body. With each inhale, see the Pentacles' yellow light inside you grow brighter and clearer. Feel the strength and power of your card, and know that that energy is inside you ready to be released.

When you feel ready, imagine yourself taking action toward your goal. Include as many sensory details of the experience as you can. Feel the position and movement of your body. Imagine the sounds that you will hear and the smells that you will smell. Allow yourself to get in touch with the emotions that your activities bring up. Once you have a clear "picture" of your total experience of working toward your goal, repeat the following affirmation to yourself:

All my actions improve my life and move me toward my abundance.

Say this affirmation to yourself 20 times. You can repeat this affirmation to yourself at any time during the day. Or write the sentence out a few times on a piece of paper. Try writing it out 20 times before you go to sleep at night. Then in the morning, before you get out of bed, write it 20 more times. You can even write your affirmation on sticky notes and attach them to your bathroom mirror, your fridge, or the dashboard of your car.

Work with your affirmation for a week or more. During that time, keep notes or write journal entries about how your feelings change. You will also want to keep records of your attitude toward the action you have committed to take and your progress toward achieving that goal. If you feel that you need another charge of Pentacle energy, do the third chakra meditation again.

Once you have completed your action, congratulate yourself! Celebrate your achievement in a way that seems right for the task you have accomplished. For a small task, you can give yourself a small reward. For a larger project, why not plan yourself a party?

When you are done celebrating, you may want to take another look at your list and see if there is another action that you can take to ease the journey along your path. If there is, commit to it now, and keep moving forward toward greater and greater prosperity and abundance.

chapter 7

Phoenix Rising: Making Your Fortune All Over Again

The Phoenix: Great bird of myth
Planetary retrogrades and their vibes
Chiron's place in Astrology and in your chart
Introducing the asteroids
Bouncing back
Enhance your prosperity corner
Tarot's Wish Spread

Your fortunes are down. Perhaps you are flat-out broke. You've spun Tarot's Wheel of Fortune, and this time you lost. But you know that sometimes you're up, and sometimes you're down. Like the Phoenix of legend, a beautiful bird that rises from the ashes of its own destruction, you will rise again. In this chapter, we will look at some more astrological influences that can affect everyone's finances and business, at how one financial high flyer created his own luck, and we provide some tips for how to increase your luck and prosperity through the use of Feng Shui, an ancient Chinese system of placement for maximum energy flow. Finally, we show you a Tarot spread that will let you know how and when your wishes for a more prosperous future will come true. Harness the Intuitive Arts of Astrology, Tarot, and Psychic Intuition and help increase your luck, prosperity, and abundance.

Rising from the Ashes

The Phoenix, a powerful symbol from mythology, represents rebirth and renewal. According to an ancient Egyptian legend, the Phoenix, a large bird with red and gold plumage, lives for 500 years. At the end of this period, it burns in its nest and then is reborn from the ashes of that fire. In ancient Rome, the ever-resurrecting Phoenix came to represent the power and constantly renewing strength of the Roman Empire. To glorify the empire, the bird's image was stamped on coins and made into mosaics. In the Chinese tradition, the Phoenix is one of the four spiritual creatures all of which are associated with a point on the compass. The direction of the Phoenix is south. Some people consider the Phoenix to represent the power of the Chinese empress. Known as Feng Huang, the Chinese Phoenix unites both *yin* and *yang* energy into a totality and is considered to be an omen of prosperity.

Your money has burned away and now you are left with just a pile of ashes. Perhaps you have overspent. Perhaps you took a stock market or real estate risk that didn't pan out. Perhaps things have just been going badly for you. Now is the time to sit back, survey your situation, plan, and then make like the Phoenix and resurrect yourself.

The ability to weather hardship is an important skill to master. Having faith in yourself and understanding that all money has its ebb and flow can help you through any financial storm. Many of us fear economic downturns and the threat of recessions. We take some comfort in knowing that larger trends affect everyone and, certainly in that respect, we really all are in this together. Lots of people have a surviving relative, an aging parent or grandparent who remembers their experience of the Great Depression. Many will tell you that, though difficult, it was the happiest time of their lives. For most people, life in those days was not about money because no one had any money. What was important was community and helping everyone stay afloat. One 94-year-old grandmother we know wishes people were more like that today. This is a great reminder that abundance and feelings of prosperity are not confined to the realm of money. You can feel your abundance in your connection to your family, friends, and community. You can also take comfort in the fact that the economy, like the Phoenix, always rises from recessions and eventually moves on to better and even booming times.

The vagaries of the stock market have certainly caused many individuals to have sleepless nights. Even the most astute business people have periods of retrenchment, but having a plan of action and sticking to it can certainly pay off. Warren Buffett is someone who knows about having a plan and following it. In 2003, *Forbes* magazine ranked Buffett the second-richest man in the world. He has been called the Oracle of Omaha and the greatest investor of all time, and he got there by sticking to his plan. During the 1990s, Buffett and his portfolio fell into disfavor. He did not follow the trend and gobble up high-tech stocks, but stuck to the tried-and-true companies he preferred, even if they didn't look like the highest-yield profitable investments available at that time.

By early 2003, after the high-tech bubble had burst, *Time* magazine touted him as the Comeback Crusader. Buffett, by following the investment strategies he has used all along and not panicking, was able to make financial gains in the face of a bear market. While everyone else's money was going south, Buffett's portfolio sparkled. He held on to the companies that he believed in, even though for the short term they were not the most profitable. Chart your own steady course, and it will carry you through the booms and the busts. An understanding of the astrological conditions that can affect the markets will help you to plan and, like Buffett, to stick to your vision.

Cycling Back: Retrogrades

In Chapter 4, we talked about the impact of the Moon ☽ as it travels through the signs of the Zodiac and the periods of time when it is void of course. Much like Moon void periods, planetary retrogrades can have an impact on your business dealings. But what does retrograde mean exactly? During a planetary retrograde, the planet in question appears to move backward in the sky. Because astrologers look at the planets from Earth and because the planets actually revolve around the Sun, there are times when the planets appear to be moving backward in the sky. When a planet is seen to be moving backward, it is retrograde. On a chart, a planet that is retrograde is marked with a symbol ℞ that looks like an R with a line drawn through its front leg.

Not surprisingly, the three planets that have the biggest impact on us here on Earth, when retrograde, are the ones that are the closest: Mercury ☿, Venus ♀, and Mars ♂. (Because the Moon orbits around the Earth, and not the Sun, it does not go retrograde.) When a planet is retrograde ℞, its energy is reversed, reconsidered, or turned inward. You can think of retrograde planets as somewhat like Tarot cards that have turned up in the reversed position. Once a planet is seen to be moving "forward" again, it is said to have gone direct and its energy flows in the more usual way.

Let's take a look at the planets and how their retrograde movement can affect you, your business, and your assets.

The Page of Swords and the Magician in their reversed positions share some of the energy of a retrograde Mercury ☿ℝ.

Each Mercury ☿ retrograde period lasts about three and a half weeks, and Mercury goes retrograde three times every year. As you can tell from the frequency of this event, it does not bring disaster or financial ruin. If it did, no business would ever survive! Rather, the Mercury retrograde period is a time to slow down and reflect. Oftentimes during the Mercury retrograde, circumstances will cause you to do just that. All the areas of life associated with Mercury will be most affected. Communications may go awry, so that the letter or information for which you have been waiting may be misdelivered, arrive late, or fail to appear at all. Your answering machine may malfunction, and your computer could very well develop a new glitch. Any travel plans you have made could encounter obstacles. You may experience flight delays or cancellations, or you may get bumped due to overbooking. The Mercury retrograde period is not a good time to buy high-tech devices, such as computers, cell phones, or DVD players. And it's an inauspicious time for signing legal papers. Contracts signed during these times often need to be renegotiated. Because everyone else is also experiencing the effects of the Mercury retrograde, it is usually quite easy to delay a contract signing or push a business meeting back until after Mercury has gone direct. If you were born during a Mercury retrograde, your thoughts and ideas will probably be rather different from those of the people around you. You probably spend a lot of time thinking and mulling over the various means of communication at your disposal. In conversation, you might either jump ahead of your fellows or trail behind them.

The Empress in the reversed position shares some of the energy of a retrograde Venus ♀R.

About every year, Venus ♀ goes retrograde for approximately six weeks. Because Venus is associated with your personal resources, this can be a great time to reconsider your personal possession needs. In the business world, Venus holds sway over relations with employees, vendors, and business partners. The Venus retrograde period is not a good time to sign contracts or initiate new undertakings. New products launched under a Venus retrograde often fail to meet sales expectations, and new companies that open their doors during these periods often lack the initial financial assets they need to get rolling. If you don't push to start new things during these periods, you can save yourself and your business time, money, and aggravation. If you were born under a Venus retrograde, you may have unconventional ideas about relationships and have a hard time fitting into the mainstream. You may feel socially awkward; but once you learn to approve of yourself, you won't feel pressure to act like anyone but yourself.

The Emperor in the reversed position shares some of the energy of a retrograde Mars ♂R.

Mars ♂, the planet of action, new starts, and get-up-and-go, goes retrograde about every other year for 10 weeks. Because all business is based on action, the movement of Mars is especially significant to your company's bottom line. You can look at this period as a timeout that will save you from rushing in and making a costly mistake. Like the Venus retrograde period, this is not a good time to introduce a new product to the market. Products released during a Mars retrograde frequently turn out not to be ready for consumer use. Often consumers don't understand the product because it is ahead of its time. Or the product's release is premature, and it suffers from technical glitches that could have been worked out had the launch been delayed. In addition, stock market prices tend to fall during these periods. So if you have investments, don't panic, and know that Mars will go direct again soon and the picture will improve. The Mars retrograde period is great for testing of products before they go to market, conducting research, assessing your personal goals and your relationship to them, and gaining clarity about your motives—both personally and in the business world. If you were born during a Mars retrograde, you can be fiercely competitive, but only with yourself. You probably have desires and ambitions that those around you do not share, and you seek your own path to fulfillment.

The Wheel of Fortune in the reversed position shares some of the energy of a retrograde Jupiter ♃ʀ.

A Jupiter ♃ retrograde occurs every 13 months and lasts for about 4 months. The Jupiter retrograde period is a time for society to slow down its movement toward growth and expansion. This is a great time for internal work to prepare yourself for future opportunities. Defining and refining your personal goals can be beneficial at this time. If you were born while Jupiter was retrograde, you may find that societal norms, values, and commonly held beliefs don't work for you. You have strong intuition and use it well to define your own meaning and value.

The World in the reversed position shares some of the energy of a retrograde Saturn ♄R.

Saturn ♄ goes retrograde every 12½ months for about 4½ months. This is a time for everyone to examine systems, rules, and organizations with an eye to revamping them so that they will work better. You may become more aware of your own power and authority during these times. Questions about your relationship to outside authorities and to society and its rules may occupy your mind. You may also become aware of how society and other people's expectations have limited you. If you were born during one of these periods, you are very aware of systems and organizational rules. You probably also have a knack for pointing out what is wrong with these structures and thus make a great reformer. The downside of being born with personal Saturn retrograde is that your extremely well-developed sense of responsibility could lead you to shoulder too much and take on the worries and tasks of others.

The Tower in the reversed position shares some of the energy of a retrograde Uranus ♅R.

A Uranus ♅ retrograde occurs for about five months every year. Under a Uranus retrograde, it's a good time to ask yourself how your own personal issues relate to changes in the world at large. You may also want to assess how much you are contributing to the betterment of society as a whole. If you were born with Uranus retrograde, you have a strong desire to rebel or to reform society. This desire may be unconscious on your part, but it is probably working under the surface much of the time. It's important for anyone with a personal Uranus retrograde to have a strong base of knowledge from which to act so that change is not carried out blindly.

The Hanged Man in the reversed position shares some of the energy of a retrograde Neptune ΨR.

Faraway Neptune Ψ moves retrograde for about five months every year. This is a great time to focus on how your own fears and issues reflect what is happening with humanity in general. It's also a great time to ask yourself if you are indulging in escapism or if you are truly acting in a positive way by, for instance, enhancing your own spirituality. If you were born with Neptune retrograde, you will have a strong need to test and question your faith. You do not accept dogma, but work toward and seek your own understanding of the spiritual path. If you are derailed from your spiritual quest, you could be seduced by drugs, alcohol, or other means of escape. Many artists, poets, musicians, and spiritual devotees were born under a retrograde Neptune.

Judgement in the reversed position shares some of the energy of a retrograde Pluto ♀R.

Super-distant Pluto ♀ is retrograde for about five months out of the year. This is the time to assess your contribution to the Earth and the evolution of mankind. If you were born under a Pluto retrograde, personal transformation and rebirth will be major points of focus for you. You will also have a need to aid in the transformation and awakening of the world as a whole and a desire to preserve the environment, the Earth, and all of its creatures.

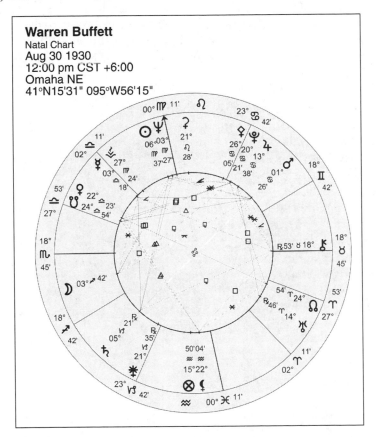

Warren Buffett, the Oracle of Omaha, was born during a number of planetary retrogrades ℞*.*

Buffett's Saturn ♄, which is retrograde ℞, is in Capricorn ♑ in his 2nd house, the house of possessions, earning abilities, and self-esteem. Saturn in Capricorn is usually the mark of a person who is ambitious and happily persistent. Saturn in this sign is determined, and it will succeed. Saturn, of course, rules Capricorn, and thus this placement lends an unswerving quality to the pursuit of goals. Hard work and discipline should come naturally to Buffett. The fact that Buffett's Saturn is in the 2nd house indicates an affinity for long-range financial planning. He makes slow and steady gains, and is in for the long haul. Saturn in the 2nd house may cause a tendency to worry about money excessively even when the individual is quite affluent. As previously mentioned, people born under a retrograde Saturn ♄℞, as Buffett was, are very aware of how systems work and want to find better ways to make them work. And Buffett is an example of this tendency—he has advocated for corporate reforms, particularly in the areas of finance and stockholder relations.

In Buffett's 5th house, the area of creativity, risk, fun, romance, and children, you will find Uranus ♅. This planet is in Aries ♈ and also is retrograde ℞. Uranus in the 5th house describes a strong need for independence and freedom. People with this planetary placement often are attracted to risks and like to express their creativity by taking a unique approach to financial investments. Uranus in Aries indicates a pioneer and a reformer, who will stick to his guns no matter what the circumstances. People born under a Uranus retrograde ♅℞, like Buffett, have an even stronger desire to reform or they feel they must rebel.

Spend some time looking over the other planets in Buffett's birth chart. Then take out your own astrological birth chart. If you have any planets in your chart that are retrograde ℞, write them down here. You also may want to make some notes about the meanings of your personal retrogrades based on the information previously discussed.

Retrograde ℞ planets in my birth chart include:

_____

_____

Chiron ⚷: A Recent Discovery

We imagine that you are wondering about some of the other symbols you see on your own birth chart and on the charts we have used throughout this book as examples.

Look back at Warren Buffett's chart. In addition to the retrograde ℞ Saturn ♄ and Uranus ♅, Buffett's Chiron ⚷ is also retrograde. You'll find it in his 7th house, the area of primary relationships and partnerships. Chiron, a planetoid that was only discovered in 1977, has much to say about relationships and can speak to financial matters as well. Chiron is named after the great centaur of Greek myth. Although the other centaurs, creatures that were half-man and half-horse, tended toward violence and ferocity, Chiron was gentle and a learned healer. Many astrologers today see Chiron's position in your birth chart as revealing your psychic wound, how you can heal yourself and then reach out to heal others as well. Other astrologers, particularly the members of the Magi Society, disagree with this interpretation and see Chiron as a key to all matters financial and romantic. For more information about this innovative view of Chiron, look for the Magi Society's book *Magi Astrology: The Key to Success in Love and Money* (Hay House, Inc., 1999) or check out their website at www.magisociety.com.

Now find your natal Chiron ⚷. Make a note of what astrological sign and house it is in. Then look for any significant aspects between your Chiron and the other planets in your chart. Buffett's Chiron is sextile Pluto ⚷ ⚹ ♇. A Magi astrologer would say that this relationship between Chiron and Pluto indicates success, power, and the ability to bring in a great deal of money through career choices—all of which sounds pretty accurate to us.

Your personal Chiron ⚷ birth chart placement is the astrological

sign of _____ in the _____ house.

Aspects to your Chiron ⚷ include:

_____

_____

More Symbols: The Asteroids

The asteroids form a belt and orbit together between Mars ♂ and Jupiter ♃. They have been given the names of Roman goddesses and are generally considered to be connected to women's issues. They can also affect your finances. Remember that Juno was the goddess of the mint in ancient Rome, and many astrologers connect Vesta with investments. Here's a table of the asteroids and their major realms of influence.

Asteroid	Realm	Areas of Influence
Ceres ⚳	Motherhood	Natural cycles, fertility, crops, relationships to parents and children
Juno ⚵	Marriage	Partnerships, contracts and agreements, social obligations
Pallas Athene ⚴	Wisdom	Intelligence, knowledge, understanding, equality
Vesta ⚶	Power	Sexuality, devotion, health, service to others

Did you notice that Warren Buffett's Juno ⚵ is retrograde ℞? You're becoming the astute and perceptive Astrology student that we knew you would!

A Comeback Yet to Come

When interviewed by *The New Yorker* in early 2003 about her legal and corporate troubles, home and garden guru Martha Stewart said, "It's sort of the American way to go up and down the ladder, maybe several times in a lifetime. And I've had a real long up." At the time of this writing, Martha is down. But we expect her, like the Phoenix, someday to rise again. Why do we think this? Martha understands the up and down, the ebb and the flow, that she will not always be the top dog, and that she does not have to stay down and remain forever the underdog, either.

In addition to her demonstrated positive attitude, Martha Stewart has a really interesting birth chart. Here you can see the way "women's issues" and finances intertwine in an astrological birth chart. Of course, the sphere of women's issues is the meat and potatoes of Martha's multifaceted business. She is all about keeping house and cooking, and, in addition to *Martha Stewart Living,* she even has a magazine called *Baby.* So let's take a look at her asteroids, the heavenly bodies of the feminine. The aspects that they make in her birth chart should outline the special nature of Martha's talents.

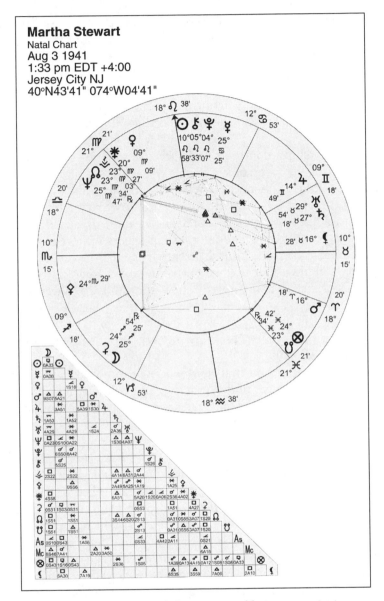

Martha Stewart
Natal Chart
Aug 3 1941
1:33 pm EDT +4:00
Jersey City NJ
40°N43'41" 074°W04'41"

Martha's asteroids reveal the nature of her prosperity.

Ceres, the asteroid associated with motherhood, is quincunx her Saturn ⚴ ⚻ ♄. Ceres is also quincunx her Mercury ⚴ ⚻ ☿. Mercury and Saturn are sextile each other ☿ ✳ ♄. So Ceres is the apex of a neat little triangle. Remember that Saturn can represent control, rules, and limitations. Mercury, of course, is all about communications and the mind. We would say, based on this alignment, that Martha has an unusual ability to control communication about motherhood. Ceres is trine Mars ⚳ △ ♂, so her mothering skills and talents get an extra boost of energy from the super-athletic warrior planet.

When we look at Martha's Juno, we find that Juno is trine Saturn ⚵ △ ♄, and that Martha is able to exert even more control, this time in the areas of partnerships, contracts and agreements, and social obligations. As a result of this control she is able to earn good money for what she does in Juno's sphere. Martha's Juno trines Uranus ⚵ △ ♅. Uranus, of course, is associated with innovation, electricity, technology, and electronics, a group that includes television and broadcasting. This planetary pairing can indicate sudden turns of events with regard to money, and can also describe unusual creativity that is rewarded with money. Are we talking about big, expensive televised wedding events? Or of Martha's ability to come up with new and innovative weddings? Both of those activities could actually be things that Martha does well. Furthermore, her Juno is conjunct Vesta ⚵ ☌ ⚶, so we have the realms of marriage and power feeding each other energy, resulting in profits and successful investments.

Pallas Athene, the asteroid that represents wisdom and holds sway over intelligence, knowledge, understanding, and equality, is trine Mercury ⚴ △ ☿. Another of Martha's talents would be to communicate her wisdom, which is just what she has done through her magazines and many TV appearances.

Vesta in Martha's chart is trine Saturn ⚶ △ ♄, and, once again, we see Martha in a position of control. She has an unusual ability to control her feminine power. Some astrologers would see this alignment as describing Martha's investments and her ability to gain money through that channel. Her Vesta also trines Uranus ⚶ △ ♅, which could again be a mark of ability to broadcast in the realm of feminine power. This alignment can speak to Martha's ability to create change or be innovative in the areas of sexuality, devotion, health, or service to others. You can also see this alignment as describing a tendency to experience sudden happenings in the realm of investments. Furthermore, Vesta is conjunct Neptune ⚶ ☌ ♆. Neptune, the planet of creativity, music, dreams, and illusion, shares energy with her asteroid of feminine power. This alignment would tend to increase Martha's girl power and at the same time make her capable of generating creative ideas, dreams, or illusions regarding both the female realm and the world of investments.

We've left a few of Martha's aspects out, but we're sure that you get the picture. We do want to point out one more set of planets, though. Notice that Martha has Saturn conjunct Uranus ♄ ☌ ♅. This alignment would indicate that she has a great deal of control over things ruled by Uranus, such as television and broadcasting. With all of her special talents, Martha is sure to do her utmost to bounce back.

All the planetary alignments in your birth chart speak of your own special abilities and talents, too. Take a moment now to review your own birth chart and aspect grid. As you focus on the aspect related to the asteroids in your chart, allow yourself to feel the power and abundance inherent in your natal gifts.

In Your Own Little Corner

Feng Shui, the ancient Chinese art of placement, can help to harmonize the energy where you live and where you work. The proper flow of energy will aid you in all your efforts and smooth your path along the road to prosperity. Feng Shui even recognizes a prosperity corner in every home and office. A properly cared for prosperity area can work wonders for your wallet. We're going to provide some suggestions for sprucing up your prosperity corner and with it the overall state of your finances.

First you need to locate your prosperity area within your house, apartment, or office. You can use one of two methods to do this. To use the first method, stand at your front door as if you have just walked in. Your prosperity area will be the room at the corner of the house, apartment, or office that is on the left and the farthest away from the door. If your space has an irregular shape, using this method can be tricky, and you may want to try method number two. To use the second method, you need to know how your home or office is situated in terms of the points of the compass. Once you have that information, this method will be easy for you. Just pick the southeast room. Remember that the south is associated with the Phoenix and the Empress. The east is traditionally associated with the Dragon and the Emperor. So it makes sense to us that the southeast would be an auspicious place full of abundant energy.

If you want to narrow your prosperity area down even further, you can combine the two methods. If you picked the far-left room of your house, use the southeast corner of that room as your prosperity corner. If you used the compass method and selected the southeast room of your house or office, stand in the doorway of that room and find your prosperity in the far-left corner of the room.

Now that you have determined where your prosperity corner is located, take a look at what is in your corner. Clutter of any sort could be negatively affecting your prosperity. Clear out any junk that may have parked itself here. Get rid of any object that is broken or worn out. Broken objects drain energy, and they are usually eyesores, too.

If there is a window adjacent to your prosperity corner, clean it. You want to have a clear view out. And why not dust the window sill and vacuum the area while you're at it?

Now you want to pick some objects to place in your prosperity corner that will enhance your abundance. In the Chinese tradition, you can place three coins or bills inside an envelope and put them in your prosperity corner to help draw more money to you. Traditionally, a red envelope is used for this purpose. In China, red, blue, and purple are all colors associated with prosperity. If your prosperity corner holds a piece of furniture, try draping it with a piece of cloth in one of these hues. Or use green if it is a color that appeals to you. A nice silk or velvet remnant can be an inexpensive way to cover a piece of furniture in luxury. (We sound like Martha!)

Alternatively, you could select a few decorative objects that make you think of and feel abundance. You could gather together a few polished stones, crystals, or semiprecious gems for your prosperity corner. Jade has long been linked to money and the drawing of wealth, and peridot, which is also known as olivine, a green stone found frequently in Hawaii, is associated both with prosperity and with the Tarot's Empress. If you know that you can keep it healthy, a thriving plant will perk up your prosperity corner. For an extra kick, bury 9 coins in the plant's pot—9 is the number of completion. As the plant grows, so will abundance increase in your life. Once you have chosen an object or objects to enhance your prosperity corner, place the object in position. Spend a few moments meditating. Allow yourself to feel the wealth of all the things you already have. Give thanks for those things. Imagine all the good that will come to you in the future, and feel gratitude for what is yet to come.

Wish Upon a Card

Tradition has it that this 15-card Wish Spread as used by gypsy fortunetellers predicts the outcome of a personal wish. The key card in this spread is the 9 of Cups—the Wish Card. When the Wish Card comes up, you know that your wish will come to pass.

Tarot's Wish Card.

To do this type of spread, first pick a card to represent you, the wisher. Or have the person whose cards you are reading pick one. Place the card in the center in the Wish position. Then shuffle the rest of the cards while thinking about your wish. Once the cards feel sufficiently shuffled, place the deck on the table face down and fan all the cards out. One at a time, draw 15 cards from the fanned-out deck. Put the rest of the deck aside. Shuffle the 15 cards that you selected and, when you feel ready, lay them out in the following pattern:

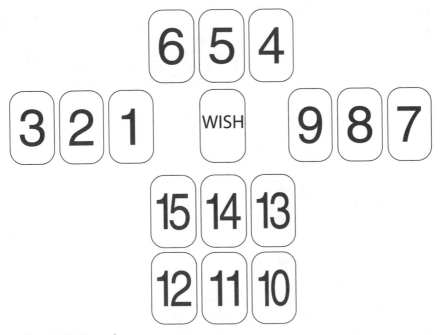

The Wish Spread.

139

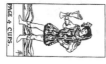

Alice's Wish Spread: Will I be able to pay off my debts this year and get out from under all these bills?

A Sample Wish Spread

Our friend Alice, who has been having a hard time financially and in other ways, too, wanted to know if she'd be able to pay off her debts this year. She wanted to try a Wish Spread to see what the cards had to say. Here is what she got:

Card Alice picked to represent herself: Temperance

This Major Arcana card represents the present focus about the issue. Alice wants to regain her balance and get back in control of her money. She wishes to develop good financial habits and maintain good discipline.

Card 1: Justice R
Card 2: 5 of Wands
Card 3: Knight of Pentacles

These first three cards represent the conditions surrounding the situation and questioner at the time of the reading and what prompted him or her to ask the particular question. These cards show that imbalance and poor handling of finances have been in Alice's past. She has experienced a loss of control over her income or her financial expenditures. This imbalance has created inner turbulence, frustration, and anxiety, which culminate in the 5 of Wands—a crisis point. The Knight of Pentacles suggests that a person offering good advice or help may approach her. This helpful person could actually be a part of herself from which she will learn to recognize and accept the good advice that comes to her.

Card 4: 9 of Swords R
Card 5: Page of Cups R
Card 6: 4 of Wands R

The goal of the question is contained in these three cards. The 9 of Swords R indicates that the sorrow and pain caused by her financial condition will slowly move away. Tomorrow will bring more hope of getting her financial situation in order. Alice has been on an emotional roller coaster (Page of Cups R), but the 4 of Wands R says that there is hope of starting to turn the situation around this year. The 4 of Wands R also can describe slow and gradual progress toward Alice's desired goal. So these cards say, there may be delays, but there will be progress.

Card 7: 10 of Cups R
Card 8: 8 of Wands R
Card 9: Wheel of Fortune

These three cards represent the oppositions or challenges to the desired goal. The 10 of Cups R indicates that Alice needs to take care of others or that an unexpected loss in her home or family will cost her more than expected. Helping other members of her family may delay the development of her own solvency. The 8 of Wands R would indicate that her goal is reachable, but may take longer than the year in question. Delays or blockages are still evident around her. The Wheel of Fortune, of course, is a good omen. Things will move in a positive direction, and Alice will have something or someone come to her aid.

Card 10: Hermit R
Card 11: 4 of Cups
Card 12: 2 of Swords

These cards represent what will come home to roost or become part of reality within the year. The Hermit R would indicate that circumstances look good, but only when Alice pays attention to wise advice and follows that advice consistently. The 4 of Cups says that Alice is looking inward and evaluating her spending habits with an eye toward changing her patterns so she does not end up in debt again. The 2 of Swords says that she will make slow progress toward her goal and that she should not get discouraged but rather listen to her inner voice and stay on the path toward her goal. Alice's attitude may need a change to keep her old patterns at bay.

Card 13: Queen of Wands
Card 14: Lovers R
Card 15: 6 of Pentacles

The last three cards show what will come into your life. The Queen of Wands will be the focus and the power behind getting out of this debt. Alice has the will, the momentum, and the concrete desire to take the bull by the horns and accomplish this task! The Lovers R says that she has to be aware of her choices. She must decide how she wants to spend her resources. If she remains conservative with her money or investments, slow and gradual progress will benefit her. In the process of her getting rid of debt, Alice will become a different person with regard to money. The 6 of Pentacles means that she can control her debt while still remaining generous toward others. She may receive help from others, or she will learn that she is able not only to pay off her debt, but to save as well.

In terms of the timing of Alice's goal, it may take her a little over a year to become debt-free. Alice had her cards read in March. Because the suit of Wands represents spring, the Lovers stand for Gemini (May 21 through June 22), and Pentacles are associated with winter, Arlene says that Alice will probably accomplish her goal between the following spring, 12 months later, and the end of winter, 18 months later.

Try your own Wish Spread now. Make sure to record your results here or in your notebook, and include the date of your reading so you can chart your progress—both in the financial realm and as a developing Tarot adept.

Date of Reading: _____

Wish Card: _____

Cards 1, 2, and 3: _____

Interpretation: _____

_____

Cards 4, 5, and 6: _____

Interpretation: _____

_____

Cards 7, 8, and 9: _____

Interpretation: _____

_____

Cards 10, 11, and 12: _____

Interpretation: _____

_____

Cards 13, 14, and 15: _____

Interpretation: _____

_____

chapter 8

Your Karmic Inheritance: Productivity Gains for Eternity

Karma in action
Imagine the abundance of the Pentacles
Nodes: More Astrology!
Find your Nodes
Tarot's Mission Spread

*It could be that you have inherited some assets and the way that
you approach your money from an earlier generation. Perhaps you
learned from your family that money was something best not discussed. Perhaps you have a legacy that has been handed down to
you from a past life. Now that we all will probably live to be 100
years old, you don't have to believe in reincarnation to see that on a
metaphorical level you will have more than one life. Whether or not
you believe in reincarnation, understanding your financial karma can
open your mind—and your portfolio—to the wisdom and beneficence
of the universe. Let's look at how Astrology, Tarot, and your Psychic
Intuition can point you toward your inheritance of wealth and happiness. Find your abundance for eternity, and watch it grow.*

Card of Success and Karma

You may think of karma as a kind of guilt that you lug around with
you from lifetime to lifetime. In this view, if you do the right things,

you may be able to work off your burden. But you don't have to believe in past lives or reincarnation to see karma at work in your present life. You may think of karma as any situation or event you encounter that you do not fully understand. Karma, then, causes you to have these same types of experiences again and again until you learn their lessons.

The word *karma* is Sanskrit, and it literally means act, deed, or work. In Hinduism and Buddhism, karma is the sum and consequences of your intentional actions throughout your existence. These experiences help to determine your fate. You can generate "good" karma through your good actions, and "bad" karma through your less-than-good behavior. To generate karma, your actions have to be intentional. Accidentally falling off your bicycle does not generate karma. Donating the bicycle that you never use to a program that benefits under-privileged children creates good karma. Intentionally running over someone else's bicycle with your car creates bad karma. (Also, it is bad for your car!)

In Chapter 6, you explored the cycle of your abundance by taking a journey through Tarot's Pentacles. Pentacles, as you know, are the cards of the financial and material world. Your travel through these cards culminated in the 10 of Pentacles, the card of success. Take the 10 of Pentacles out from your deck now and place it in front of you.

The 10 of Pentacles depicts security and stability—a great legacy to leave behind.

When this card comes up for you in a reading, it says: Success is yours! When we look at this card, we also see all the good karma that this family has accumulated. In the West, we often mistakenly think of the ideals from Eastern cultures as being ones of asceticism or deprivation. Certainly, those strains do exist in Eastern cultures, and they are practiced by a select few. For most people, though, the goal is to properly understand one's place in relation to the self, the family, and society and to maintain a way of life in which moral, mental, and ethical attainments all come together. Karma yoga describes work that is initiated from a place of unselfishness—not for your own benefit, but for the good of others and for the world as a whole. For example, if you owned a factory and focused on the impact of your plant on the environment, the well-being of your customers and employees, and the long-term benefits to society that you could generate, instead of focusing on the short-term goals of making a name for yourself in the industry and collecting profits, you would be giving of yourself and practicing karma yoga.

Doesn't it look as if the people on the 10 of Pentacles have been working to improve life for everyone? Well, it feels that way to us. Not only does the card represent a high level of financial security, the entire family has worked to secure the future of all its members. Even the future grandchildren of the little boy on the card will benefit from the stable foundation that this family has built. And society as a whole will benefit, too. This family is not just passing down wealth to the next generation. They are also handing down a tradition of hard work, independence, pride in a job well done, service, a caring attitude, and a sensible relationship to money. Whether you believe in reincarnation or not, you certainly believe in what you are building. The financial stability that you create today will be your gift to the generations of your family to come; and if you do have a next life, that extra cash (and karma) sure will come in handy!

The 10 of Pentacles in the reversed position shows a family in conflict and in danger of losing their assets.

In the reversed position, the 10 of Pentacles depicts a family in strife, and they are probably fighting over their money or investments. This conflict could very well ruin any financial stability that they have achieved. But it is not just money that is at stake here. The good karma of the entire family is at risk, too. If this card in the reversed position comes up for you in a reading, take it as a warning and check how you can take extra care of your assets and your family relations.

Join the Pentacle Family

Get out your notebook and a pen. Examine the image on the 10 of Pentacles. Make sure to turn the card upright again, if you have turned it over. Now, pick one person on the card. Imagine that you are that person, and without thinking about it too much, spend 10 minutes writing down everything that you know about yourself as the person on the card. You might start by describing your clothes, your likes and dislikes, your fears or your hopes for the future. You might write about your emotional state as captured in the present moment of the card or about how the garland of flowers feels resting on your head.

Write as fast as you can, don't stop, don't read what you are writing, and don't lift your pen from the page. It is okay if you repeat things that you have already written. It is also okay if you write something that seems weird, inaccurate, or downright wrong to your rational side. It is also okay if you write, "What should I say?" or "What else?" Just keep writing. Your goal here is to busy your mind (and hand) so that you can connect to your Psychic Intuition.

After your 10 minutes are up, read over what you have written. Read with a sense of discovery, as if this were a treasure hunt and you are searching for the keys to your own personal treasure. As you wrote, were you able to connect to the abundance of the card? You may want to highlight any passages that strike you as interesting or surprising. If you come across a passage you particularly like, use your favorite pen and copy it out in your best handwriting on a sheet of nice paper. Or type it into your computer, put it in a font you like, print it out, and post it somewhere important—like in your prosperity corner. You may want to use one of your sentences as a jumping-off point for a story, a painting, a collage, or a dance—it's all about your abundance, after all. Can you use these words, thoughts, feelings, or images to help unlock your own treasure?

Perhaps you found yourself moving in a different direction. If what you have written seems whiny or negative, look at it closely. Do the beliefs and attitudes expressed sound like you, or do they sound like something that has been handed down to you? Can you identify from whom the voice and the negative sentiments come? Sometimes, even after we think that we have left them behind, we unconsciously mimic the beliefs and attitudes of our family of origin. Now, take a negative statement, if you have one, and turn it into a positive affirmation. For example, say at the beginning of this exercise you picked the woman wearing the garland of flowers, and you wrote: "I hate these flowers. Why can't I have a hat? I never get what I want." You could turn "I never get what I want" into "I am gifted by the universe with all that I desire" or "I meet my needs and desires easily." Remember that you want your affirmation to be in the present tense, as if it describes what is actually happening now. You also want to keep the language of your affirmation positive, so avoid negatives such as "not," "no," or "never."

Once you have developed an affirmation, write it out 20 times in your notebook. If you feel so moved, make a little poster of your affirmation and put it up in your prosperity corner. Say your affirmation over to yourself as you go about your day, and see if you can create a new inheritance for yourself and for future generations.

Astrology's Nodes: North ☊ and South ☋

The Nodes ☊ ☋ of the Moon ☽, moving points that relate to the Moon's orbit around the Earth, can be keys to understanding your financial karma. The placement of these lunar signs represents your past and your future—both in this life and in your lives to come. Looked at together, they describe the activities and events that will be easy for you, and the life challenges you will need to meet and master in order to grow. The symbols used to represent the Nodes are also known as the dragon's head ☊ and the dragon's tail ☋. We like to think of this dragon as bounding toward an abundant future with its tail streaming back into the past it has just left behind.

Your South Node ☋ (dragon's tail) describes the lessons that you have learned in your past lives, either actual or metaphorical. The wisdom from these lessons may manifest itself as skills, talents, or an affinity for certain types of people. You'll be drawn to people and situations that reflect your South Node because they will feel familiar. In this respect, your South Node represents your comfort zone. The lessons of the South Node still apply to you and your life, but you've incorporated them into your daily existence already.

Your North Node ☊ (dragon's head) indicates karmic lessons that you haven't yet mastered. Facing the challenge of your North Node route isn't as easy as following your South Node path, but if you choose to accept its challenges, your striving will bring you the fulfillment of self-actualization as well as the rewards of abundance and connection to the world around you.

When we look at the Nodes astrologically, we look at them together, because they always oppose each other in a birth chart. If you think of the Nodes as the head and tail of the dragon, this will make perfect mythological sense—the dragon stretches across your chart, and where the head is, the tail must follow! From a philosophical point of view, the Nodes describe two sides of a coin—what you know and have mastered already (tails!), and on the flip side (heads!), the challenge of what you have yet to learn. Now let's look at the Nodal dyads in each sign.

If your **North Node ☊ is in Aries ♈** and your **South Node ☋ is in Libra ♎**, your challenge is to learn to be independent, take the initiative, and feel confidence in yourself and your earning power. You've already learned about cooperation and have integrated skills relating to cooperation and the ability to work with others into your life.

If your **North Node ☊ is in Taurus ♉** and your **South Node ☋ is in Scorpio ♏**, your challenge is to learn about material values. Once you have truly learned that the universe will provide for you, you will be able to create a stable and harmonious home. You've already learned about power, the power of transformation and, possibly, the occult, and have integrated your esoteric knowledge into your daily life.

If your **North Node ☊ is in Gemini ♊** and your **South Node ☋ is in Sagittarius ♐**, your challenge is to learn new communication skills that you can use on the job and you need to learn to see both sides of a fiscal issue. You've already learned about freedom and the pursuit of truth and have integrated your philosophical outlook into your daily activities.

If your **North Node ☊ is in Cancer ♋** and your **South Node ☋ is in Capricorn ♑**, your challenge is to learn to share your emotions about money, to be sensitive to others, and to nurture. You've already learned about responsibility and achievement, and you know how to use your sense of ambition to get what you want.

If your **North Node ☊ is in Leo ♌** and your **South Node ☋ is in Aquarius ♒**, your challenge is to learn about generosity and how to share your resources, both the material and the inner ones such as love, with others. You've already learned the value of detachment and have mastered a type of innovation or the more valuable aspects of eccentricity.

If your **North Node** ☊ is **in Virgo** ♍ and your **South Node** ☋ is **in Pisces** ♓, your challenge is to learn to be practical and discerning in your dealings with others. You've already learned to be compassionate and have a strong sense both of your intuition and of other people's feelings.

If your **North Node** ☊ is **in Libra** ♎ and your **South Node** ☋ is **in Aries** ♈, your challenge is to learn to cooperate and work with other people. You've already learned to lead, and are able to be independent and take the initiative, while maintaining your self-confidence.

If your **North Node** ☊ is **in Scorpio** ♏ and your **South Node** ☋ is **in Taurus** ♉, your challenge is to learn about power, transformation, and maybe even the occult sciences. You've already learned about material values and the importance of a stable, harmonious, and beautiful home.

If your **North Node** ☊ is **in Sagittarius** ♐ and your **South Node** ☋ is **in Gemini** ♊, your challenge is to seek the truth and find a philosophy that harmonizes with your daily life. You've already learned how to communicate with others and are usually aided in your endeavors by your ability to see both sides of an issue.

If your **North Node** ☊ is **in Capricorn** ♑ and your **South Node** ☋ is **in Cancer** ♋, your challenge is to learn about responsibility, the harnessing of ambition, and achievement. You've already learned about nurturing, are sensitive, and are able to share your emotions with others.

If your **North Node** ☊ is **in Aquarius** ♒ and your **South Node** ☋ is **in Leo** ♌, your challenge is to learn to be generous to all and use your skills and resources for the betterment of all humankind. You've already learned how to be generous to those you care about and are both loving and creative.

If your **North Node** ☊ is **in Pisces** ♓ and your **South Node** ☋ is in **Virgo** ♍, your challenge is to learn to be understanding and compassionate and to develop your intuition. You've already learned to be practical, analytical, and discerning when it comes to the people and issues that you encounter in your daily life.

Now let's look at the significance of the Nodal pairs in each of the astrological houses. Remember that the houses represent the different areas of your life.

If your **North Node** ☊ is **in the 1st house** and your **South Node** ☋ is **in the 7th house,** you need to develop your leadership skills. You probably have a natural tendency to fade into the background, and you often allow the business of others to take over your time. If you wish to grow, you need to examine who you really are, and then, with your own needs in mind, step forward and start along the path to your own abundance.

If your **North Node ☊** is **in the 2nd house** and your **South Node ☋** is **in the 8th house,** you need to establish values of your own and learn to live by them. Remember that the 2nd house is associated with resources and money earned, while the 8th house is concerned with shared resources and money derived from others. You've already learned how to adapt to the values of others in order to get by and you are adept at keeping secrets. If you wish to grow, you need to work to determine what is truly meaningful to you, learn about your own earning potential, and begin to put your own financial plans into action.

If your **North Node ☊** is **in the 3rd house** and your **South Node ☋** is **in the 9th house,** you need to work on your communication and relationship skills. You've already acquired much knowledge and even wisdom; but to grow, you need to be able to communicate what you know to others.

If your **North Node ☊** is **in the 4th house** and your **South Node ☋** is **in the 10th house,** you need to learn to build a harmonious and nurturing foundation for both your home and your career. Chances are, you know how to establish your authority; but to grow, you need to temper your concern with rules and status and cultivate comfortable roots.

If your **North Node ☊** is **in the 5th house** and your **South Node ☋** is **in the 11th house,** you need to learn to establish realistic goals and follow through to achieve them. You already know how to dream up creative visions. If you want to grow, you need to learn to act on your plans.

If your **North Node ☊** is **in the 6th house** and your **South Node ☋** is **in the 12th house,** you need to learn to trust the universe and the other people in it. Chances are, you feel most comfortable in the world of your own mind; but if you wish to grow, you need to look at what is real. Then you can share your compassion and be of service to others.

If your **North Node ☊** is **in the 7th house** and your **South Node ☋** is **in the 1st house,** you need to learn to cooperate with others, both at work and at home. You already know about individuality and self-expression; but to grow, you need to learn to share your strength and help others see their own true value.

If your **North Node** ☊ is **in the 8th house** and your **South Node** ☋ is **in the 2nd house,** you need to learn self-control, particularly in the realm of money and possessions. Chances are, you already know all about your own value system, earning abilities, and what you think things are worth; but to grow, you need to consider the values of others, learn to share your resources, and step away from your possibly excessive behavior.

If your **North Node** ☊ is **in the 9th house** and your **South Node** ☋ is **in the 3rd house,** you need to learn to move beyond the dramas of the everyday. Chances are, you listen to many different people and their stories; but if you wish to grow, you need to look at the big picture and work toward your connection to your intuition and higher spiritual mind.

If your **North Node** ☊ is **in the 10th house** and your **South Node** ☋ is **in the 4th house,** you need to learn responsibility—to your self and to others—and establish a career. Chances are, your family tugs at you when you set off on your path; but for you to grow, you must rise above family problems and feel your own dignity outside of the home.

If your **North Node** ☊ is **in the 11th house** and your **South Node** ☋ is **in the 5th house,** you need to learn objectivity so you can use your creativity to help the global community. You've already learned to be proud of your creative efforts; but to grow, you need to learn the value of input from others.

If your **North Node** ☊ is **in the 12th house** and your **South Node** ☋ is **in the 6th house,** you need to learn to see yourself as a part of the universe as a whole and at the same time understand that the universe is contained within you. You already know about self-sacrifice at the office, and have even pushed yourself in unhealthy ways. If you wish to grow, you need to move beyond workaholism and toward true service.

The Nodes in Action

Now let's take a look at the Nodes, their signs, and their positions within the houses in Oprah Winfrey's natal chart.

Oprah's North Node ☊ is in Capricorn ♑, and her South Node ☋ is in Cancer ♋. This configuration would indicate that she has already learned how to nurture both herself and others. She has a natural sensitivity, and is in touch both with her own emotions and with those of others. We would say that this is very true of Oprah, and her emotional openness has been one of the keys to her success. Oprah's North Node ☊ presents her challenge in this life, which is to learn about achievement, ambition, and responsibility, both to herself and to others.

It's interesting to note that her South Node is conjunct Uranus ☋ ☌ ♅, and Uranus is in its natural house, which would indicate that innovation and marching to her own drummer are perhaps familiar to her from past lives or are at least a part of her present-day comfort zone.

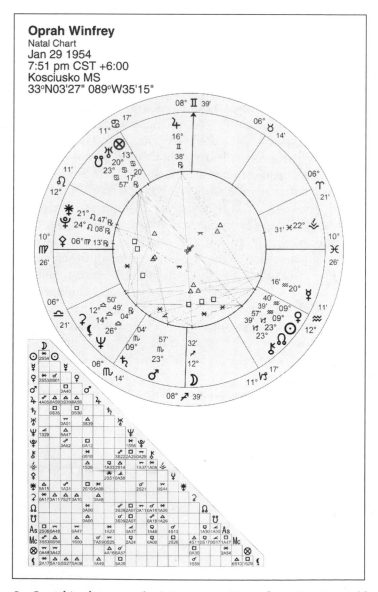

In Oprah's chart, we find the North Node ☊ in Capricorn ♑ and the South Node ☋ in Cancer ♋.

We would say that Oprah has been doing an excellent job of shouldering the responsibility of her North Node ☊ challenge. Not only has she worked her way out of a childhood of poverty to become the first woman to own and produce her own national talk show, but she is also the first African American woman to become a billionaire. And Oprah has not just accumulated wealth for herself. In 2000, she created Oprah's Angel Network, which began distributing $100,000 "Use Your Life Awards" to individuals who are working to improve the lives of others. Her acts of charity have helped to increase her success, too. Suze Orman, the financial guru, contributing editor to Oprah's magazine, and best-selling author, has pointed out that her clients who regularly give to charity end up being more successful financially than those who don't, regardless of how much money they start out with. So it appears that whatever you give really does come back to you many times over.

Oprah has said that her biggest challenge, the thing that she still needs to work on, and the thing that comes up for her over and over again, has been to learn to say "no." Now that sounds like a karmic lesson! Knowing how to set limits and say "no" when appropriate is part of your responsibility to yourself. So we say to Oprah, go ahead and say "no," and continue to work to meet your North Node challenge!

In terms of the houses, Oprah's North Node ☊ occupies her 5th house, the area of creativity, risk, fun, romance, and children. Remember that the 5th house is associated with the Sun ☉ and the sign of Leo ♌. Her South Node ☋ sits in her 11th house, which is associated with Uranus ♅ and the sign of Aquarius ♒ and is all about goals, groups, and friends. So we see that her North Node ☊ challenge is connected to her creativity, learning to set goals and follow through, and taking appropriate financial risks, which she has been doing. The fact that her Sun ☉ is in the house of its natural rulership and is conjunct her North Node ☊ would tend to heighten the energy of both her challenge and her ability to rise to it. It's interesting to note that in interviews she has often mentioned her desire to continue acting, and that she started her own production company to give herself opportunities as an actress. Perhaps part of her challenge now is to follow through with that plan and make her acting dreams more of a reality.

Because we are concerned with finances and personal resources, let's take a moment to look at Oprah's 2nd house, the area of possessions, earning ability, and self-esteem. The 2nd house is naturally associated with Taurus ♉ and thus is ruled by Venus ♀. Notice that Libra ♎ is on Oprah's 2nd house cusp. So the ruler of her 2nd house is also Venus. Furthermore, Venus in Oprah's chart is located in her 5th house, the area of creativity, and is conjunct her Sun ♀ ♂ ☉. Clearly, Oprah's creativity plays a huge role in her karmic mission in terms both financial and personal.

Ted Turner is another self-made billionaire. The owner of Turner Broadcasting and CNN, Ted was, at one point, worth $6.9 billion. Ted got his start in business after his father's suicide in 1963, when he took over the bankrupt family business. He managed to raise enough money to buy a few sports teams, and he organized the first Goodwill Games in Moscow in 1986. Interspersed with all his business activity, he has campaigned against nuclear weapons and supported a variety of causes, including peace activism, population control, and environmentalism. Ted is not a stranger to philanthropy either. In 1997, he donated one billion dollars to the United Nations. At the time of this writing, though, many of Ted's investments had lost a great deal of value. Rumor had it that he was down to his last billion. In March 2003, Ted explained to a reporter at *Business Week* why it was that he had offered to go to Iraq as a CNN war correspondent: "I'm 64 and pretty well wiped out [financially] anyway. I might as well go down in flames." Well, we're not sure that Ted is totally wiped out, and we suspect that he, too, will bounce back; but let's take a look at his birth chart and the placement of his North and South Nodes to determine what Ted's Nodal challenge is.

Ted's North Node ☊ is in Scorpio ♏ and his South Node ☋ is in Taurus ♉. So Ted has already learned about material values and the importance of a stable, harmonious, and beautiful home. His North Node is challenging him to learn about power, transformation, and maybe even the occult sciences. Could it be that Ted needs to buy a copy of this book? His nodal placement suggests that material loss would upset him greatly. The comfort and security of the home, represented by his Taurian South Node, is where he is coming from. Facing his North Node challenge even—we should say especially—in the face of tough economic times will help him feel more secure.

Ted's North Node ☊ is in the 11th house, the area of goals, groups, and friends, and his South Node ☋ is in the 5th house. So he needs to learn objectivity so he can use his creativity to help the global community. We think it is interesting that Ted's North Node ☊, which in the sign of Scorpio ♏ is speaking about power, transformation, and the occult, is situated in the house naturally ruled by Uranus ♅, the planet associated with innovation, electronics, broadcasting, and TV. Could it be that Ted needs to create a new television show dealing with transformation, rebirth, and the power of karma? But if you look further, you'll see that in addition, Ted's Uranus, like Oprah's, is conjunct ♂ his South

Node. So perhaps television as we know it is too much a part of Ted's past and his comfort zone. Could his North Node be challenging him to create a new form of broadcasting altogether?

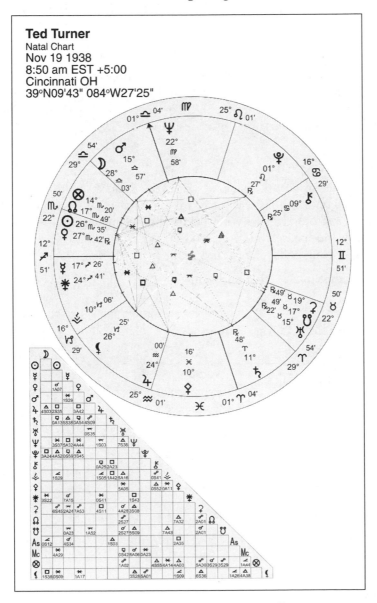

*In Ted Turner's birth chart, the North Node ☊ is in
Scorpio ♏, and the South Node ☋ is in Taurus ♉.*

Ted's 2nd house, the area of possessions, earning abilities, and self-esteem, is ruled by Saturn, the planet of rules and limitation. His Venus ♀, the natural ruler of the 2nd house, is in the 12th house, the area of the subconscious, karma, privacy, and psychic visions. Although his Venus is not conjunct his North Node, they do share the sign of Scorpio ♏. And, just as in Oprah's chart, Ted's Venus is conjunct his Sun ♀ ☌ ☉. Furthermore, Ted's North Node is only about 11 degrees away from his Sun. So Ted's possessions, earning abilities, and self-esteem are also related to his North Node challenge to learn about the spiritual and the transformative. Do you feel Ted, driven by his North Node dragon head, lurching into the New Age?

Know Your Nodes

Now it's time for you to find out what your Nodes say about you and your challenge. You'll also want to take a look at your second house, its ruler in your chart, and your Venus ♀ placement. Take out your birth chart and locate your Nodes ☊ ☋. Write down the signs and houses that your nodes fall in and make note of your Nodal challenge.

North Node ☊, sign and house: _____

_____

South Node ☋, sign and house: _____

_____

Your Nodal challenge: _____

_____

To find your 2nd house ruler, locate the sign on the cusp of your 2nd house. Remember that each sign has a planetary ruler.

In case it is not fresh in your mind, here's a table of the signs and their natural rulers:

Astro Sign	Natural Ruler
Aries ♈	Mars and Pluto ♂, ♀
Taurus ♉	Venus ♀
Gemini ♊	Mercury ☿
Cancer ♋	Moon ☽
Leo ♌	Sun ☉
Virgo ♍	Mercury ☿

Astro Sign	Natural Ruler
Libra ♎	Venus ♀
Scorpio ♏	Pluto and Mars ♀, ♂
Sagittarius ♐	Jupiter ♃
Capricorn ♑	Saturn ♄
Aquarius ♒	Uranus and Saturn ♅, ♄
Pisces ♓	Neptune and Jupiter ♆, ♃

Your 2nd house sign: _____

Your 2nd house ruler: _____

Now look and see if your North Node challenge relates to your 2nd house area of personal resources. It may, but it also may not. Either way, now that you know what your Nodal challenge is you should have a better understanding of the actions that you need to take to feel abundant and whole. You may also have a much clearer view on why certain issues seem to pop up in your life over and over again. That's karma for you!

More Karma in the Cards

Let's use the Tarot to help you look at your money karma further. The Mission Spread can show you what approach to money you may have inherited from past lives or from your family. You can think of your past life as a previous incarnation, or you can think of your past life as just the regular old past, when you may have felt like a different person. Now that we will all live to be 100, we will all, in the course of one lifetime, have past lives!

The Mission Spread can help you refine your goals and develop good habits. If you accept the present mission that life presents you, you will have a new—and a more full and abundant—life whether you believe in reincarnation or not. Your Mission Spread can also help to steer you on the path to building abundance for yourself and for the next generation as well. If you are having trouble getting yourself motivated to deal with your financial issues for your own sake, perhaps you will find it easier to work to improve your position in order to better the lot of others— either members of your own family or society at large. And know, too, that your future abundance is not just about money, but can include your home, your attitudes—your sense of satisfaction, your work ethic, your generosity—and your knowledge and understanding of the deeper issues connected to money and personal finance.

If you don't know what your mission is in relation to abundance, Tarot's Mission Spread can help you discover the answer. In a Mission Spread, you use 21 cards to clarify your past, present, and future mission and purpose regarding a specific question. You might, for example, ask what kind of work would both make you happy and bring you profit, how you can best eliminate debt from your life, or how you can change your attitude and open up to the abundance around you.

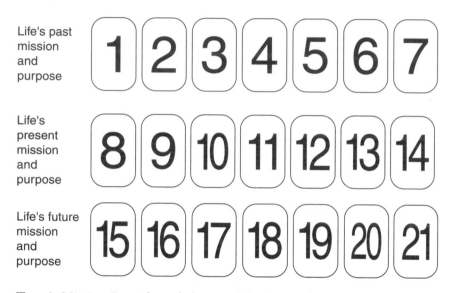

Tarot's Mission Spread can help you discover your purpose in the financial realm.

The top row of cards in a Mission Spread represents the actions that you have taken so far with regards to your question, or, to put it another way, this particular mission's past, which can include what you have inherited from the past, or even your financial abundance in a past life. The middle row concerns your present mission—what you're doing now (or should be doing) to make your mission fruitful. The bottom row shows your mission's future—both the events that could occur and actions or attitudes you can effect to make sure that they do. You can see this future influence for this life, or perhaps a future life, if you believe in reincarnation. Unlike many other Tarot spreads, the cards in each row of a Mission Spread should be read together as a group rather than individually.

To start discovering your financial purpose, first formulate a question that you would like your Mission Spread to answer. Write down your question here:

_____

Shuffle your Tarot deck while you think about your question. Shuffle until you feel the cards have an answer for you. If you like, cut the deck. Then place the cards in formation, dealing out seven cards for each row.

Give yourself a moment to gaze at the spread as a whole. Then start to examine the first row of cards—your past mission and purpose regarding the question. Once you feel you have received the message of the first row, move on to the second row. There you will find described where you are now—your present mission and purpose. When you are ready, move on to the bottom row and learn about your question's future mission and purpose. Use the space below to record your initial impressions, or record the cards from the reading and make interpretive notes in your journal.

Past: _____

Present: _____

Future: _____

After you've finished studying your Mission Spread, don't put it away. Get out some paper, pens, crayons, colored pencils, pastels, or paint—any medium that you like to work with. Or grab a few magazines that you can cut up for a collage. To help you integrate the new information you have gained from your spread, you are going to create an image for each of the three rows of cards. So the first image will represent your past and your inheritance with regard to the issue. The second image will be about your present as it has been reflected to you in the cards. And your third image will illustrate your future mission and purpose.

Put on some music to listen to while you work. If some of the images from the cards are particularly resonant for you, incorporate those features into your picture. You could draw your version of one of the cards. Or you could home in on a particular feature that has significance for you. Alternatively, you could go completely abstract and illustrate a feeling state without any concretely represented objects. Feel free to add actual objects to your illustration. You may want to include yarn, string, small stones, shells, or feathers. Have as much fun with this exercise as you can!

chapter 9

Create Your Abundance Portfolio

Transits: Knowing your opportunities
Progressions mean progress
Another event chart
Your Intuitive Arts abundance portfolio
A day of abundance
Your abundance bottom line
Enhance your prosperity—and its corner
Your abundance and the world

While reading this book, you have learned a lot about the Intuitive Arts. You've also learned a lot about yourself and your relationship to your own abundance. It's time to pull all that knowledge together. First, you are going to take a look at astrological transits and how you can capitalize on them. You'll take another look at progressions, too, and you'll study another super-successful event chart with an eye on how you can best profit from the movements of the heavenly spheres. Then, by combining your skills of Astrology, Tarot, and Psychic Intuition, you'll map out where you are and where you want to go. In addition, you'll compile your personal balance sheet, and finally we leave you with some ideas for how you can stay inspired and keep progressing on the Intuitive Arts path toward abundance.

Heavenly Bodies in Motion: Transits

Over time your abundance will be affected by a number of factors. One factor that we have touched on is your astrological transits. In Chapter 5, we looked at the challenges and opportunities that the Saturn return and the Pluto transit can bring. Of course, all the other planets in the sky do transit the heavens and form significant aspects with the planets in your birth chart. We see these celestial events as opportunities for growth and profit. Even the Saturn return and the Pluto □ Pluto, which may not be the most fun times you have ever had, can bring with them many changes for the better.

Mercury ☿ = Communication. As the innermost planet of our solar system, Mercury moves really fast. In one month, this speedy planet can leave one sign, cross through another, and start to enter the third. So a Mercury transit may last only a day or two. Because Mercury is the planet of communication and is also associated with thought and travel, all you writers and travel agents out there may want to keep an eye out for Mercury's movements in the sky. For example, Mercury transiting your natal Mercury in a trine ☿ △ ☿ can give you extra speed and power in the verbal department, and that might be just the thing you need to write that annual report for work. Mercury transiting to conjunct your natal Venus ☿ ☌ ♀ can add beauty to your expression and says that you could gain some money from using your golden voice. Mercury transiting your natal Jupiter ♃ can enhance the logic and wisdom of anything that you write or say (or sing, for that matter) while you are under the transit.

Venus ♀ = Self-worth. Another fast-moving planet, a Venus transit may last for just a few days. A conjunction ☌, sextile ⚹, or trine △ from transiting Venus can bring you quick additions to your personal possessions and earning abilities, such as freelance jobs. This is also a great time to start any type of new business, and it helps you look and feel great, too.

Mars ♂ = Energy. Because Mars's energy can be very aggressive, transits from Mars, although they bring lots of zap, are not always helpful to your business. Mars making a nice angle to your natal Mercury ☿ could help you get things done in any of the fields ruled by Mercury. In addition, Mars transiting your natal Pluto ♇ in a conjunction ☌, sextile ⚹, or trine △ can help your business endeavors to be profitable.

Jupiter ♃ = Expansion. Jupiter just makes everything better. Under most Jupiter transits—conjunction ☌, sextile ⚹, or trine △—you will feel good. Jupiter tends to enhance the energy of whatever planet it is transiting in your chart. It also adds an element of wisdom. So if you need to start something and you have a beneficial Jupiter transit coming up, wait till the planets align, and allow Jupiter to help you.

Saturn ♄ = Challenge. Some astrologers define Saturn transits as times of great learning. Saturn can push you to let go of the old and change. It can also add a measure of control to the energies represented by the planet being transited. Other astrologers look at Saturn as a marker for loss.

Uranus ♅ = Change. The way that you view a Uranus transit is going to depend on how you feel about change. Some of you may find it thrilling, while others of you will want to dig in your heels or hide under the bed. Uranus making a nice angle—conjunction ☌, sextile ✶, or trine △ to your Sun ☉, can be a great time to deal with large groups of people, innovations, or electronics.

Neptune ♆ = Dreams. A Neptune transit can cause you to reevaluate your dreams and question what it is that you want. Neptune, of course, is slow moving and very far away from the Earth. As a result, it may not be clear to your conscious mind exactly how or why you are questioning. Because Neptune is also associated with inspiration and creativity, these can be exciting times full of new and profitable ideas.

Pluto ♀ = Transformation. Do you want to turn that pile of straw into gold? When Pluto is making a conjunction ☌, sextile ✶, or trine △ to Venus ♀, you just might be able to do that. This is a great time for money-making ventures, starting a job, or opening a mutual fund. Any of the nice aspects of transiting Pluto can help turn your straw into gold—these are great times for making money. Pluto squares □ and oppositions ☍, on the other hand, can leave you high and dry and with a big pile of dusty straw to boot. Avoid starting a new job or business, or opening a new account under a Pluto square or opposition.

Progressions of Progress

You took a quick look at Karyn's progressed chart in Chapter 6. The outer wheel of a progressed chart shows your progress—how you have grown and matured. In a progressed chart, the faster-moving planets will show more change and the slower ones, such as Jupiter ♃, Saturn ♄, Uranus ♅, and Pluto ♀, will appear to have hardly budged.

Let's take a look at Oprah Winfrey's progressed chart for April 17, 2000—the day that she launched her hugely successful *O: The Oprah Magazine.*

Notice that Oprah's Sun ☉ has gone from the 5th house in Aquarius ♒ in her birth chart and progressed to the 7th house in Pisces ♓ in her progressed chart. Her progressed Pluto ♀ and Pallas Athene ♀ are making a quincunx ⚻ to Oprah's natal Chiron ⚷ and to her South Node ☋. The Pluto-Chiron quincunx ♀ ⚻ ⚷ is considered by some astrologers to be the mark of an enterprise that will be super-profitable. Quincunxes, though, are mostly seen as mixed blessings; they can impart a quality of genius, but they also demand certain adjustments. What's especially interesting to note here is that Oprah's progressed Venus ♀, which is in Aries ♈, is sextile ✳ her midheaven. Venus, of course, can be representative of women, and Aries is associated with new beginnings. So what better time to launch a new women's magazine? Remember, too, that the midheaven is located on the cusp of the 10th house, the area associated with career and reputation. We were also interested to see that Chiron ⚷ is making steady progress toward Oprah's natal Sun ☉. It's only moved about four degrees since the time of her birth; but as it approaches her Sun, Oprah's business will only prosper and her great charisma increase. So in Oprah's case it really is true—she's not getting older, she's getting better.

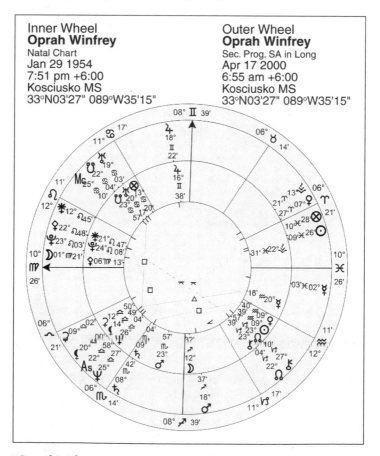

Oprah's chart progressed to the day that she launched her magazine O.

A Launch That Was an Event

What is often more illuminating than progressions, which can be subtle, is looking at transits. Examining Oprah's astrological transits on the day that her magazine launched certainly sheds some light on its huge success. Hailed by *The New York Times* as the "most successful new magazine in decades," copies of O sold out nationwide. Here is Oprah's chart with her transits for O's launch date around the outside.

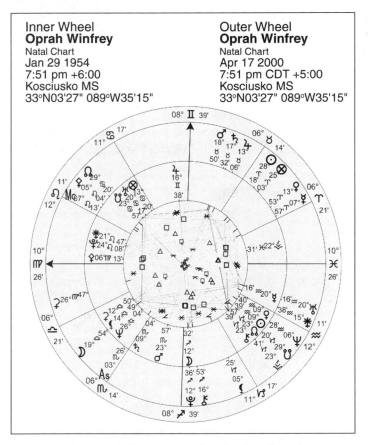

Oprah's chart with her transits for the day that she launched her magazine O.

Notice that transiting Pluto is making a conjunction with Oprah's natal Moon ♀ ☌ ☽ in Sagittarius ♐. This is a great aspect to have. As Arlene put it, "That is what Pluto can do—make you even more famous!" Notice, too, that transiting Uranus is lined up in a perfect conjunction with her natal Mercury ♅ ☌ ☿ in Aquarius ♒. This would tend to give the day for Oprah an energy of innovation, especially in the area of communications. Also, transiting Uranus makes a quincunx to her natal Uranus ♅ ⚻ ♅. This transit probably brought a quality of revolutionary genius to the magazine, but required adjustments on the part of those involved. Perhaps this transit would explain the early turnover in O's editorial staff. The transiting Moon, which is in Libra ♎, is trining Oprah's natal Mercury ☽ △ ☿, which would tend to give a serene emotional energy to communication. All in all, we would say this launch was quite an event!

You can use Astrology in planning your own events, such as the launch of a magazine, the founding of a business, the opening of a mutual fund portfolio, starting a new job, or signing a contract. If you know that you have beneficial transits on the horizon, you can plan all of your personal business so that the stars aid you in your endeavors and speed along your success and nurture your abundance.

Your Intuitive Arts Abundance Portfolio

As you know, each house of your astrological chart represents a different area of your life. The 2nd house is all about your possessions, earning abilities, and self-esteem, while the 6th house relates to work. You also know that abundance is not just about money. Your feelings of abundance (or lack thereof) pervade every aspect of your life—from dealing with your assets to interacting with family and friends, from using and feeding your own creativity and knowledge to your productivity and sense of worth at work.

In this exercise, you combine Astrology, Tarot, and your Psychic Intuition to look at each area of life represented by the astrological houses as they relate to your abundance. First get out your Tarot deck, a pen, and your notebook. Find a clear surface where you can spread out all the cards and look at them. Clear off the kitchen table and really give yourself room to stretch out. Or you may want to sprawl on the floor if this is comfortable for you.

Starting with the 1st house, pick a card for each area of life represented by the houses. To do this, repeat the keyword descriptions for each house as you look through the cards, and add the phrase "as it relates to my abundance." For example, while looking for your 1st house card, you would say, "My physical self as it relates to my abundance, my personality as it relates to my abundance, my identity as it relates to my abundance, my early childhood as it relates to my abundance." Keep repeating these phrases over and over to yourself to keep your rational mind busy and allow your Psychic Intuition to kick in and select your 1st house card. You may be able to pick a card fairly quickly, or it may take longer than you think it should. Be patient with yourself, repeat the keywords, and the right card will surface. Put the card aside and move on to the next house. Here is a list of keywords for each house.

House	Keywords
1st	Physical self, personality, identity, early childhood
2nd	Possessions, earning abilities, self-esteem
3rd	Knowledge, communication, siblings, environment
4th	Home, family, foundation of life
5th	Creativity, risk, fun, romance, children
6th	Personal responsibilities, health, work, service
7th	Primary relationships, partnerships
8th	Joint resources, sex, death, transformation, and rebirth
9th	Education, travel, philosophy, ideals, religion, law
10th	Reputation, career, social responsibilities
11th	Goals, groups, friends
12th	Subconscious, karma, privacy, psychic vision

Once you have selected a card for your 1st house, move on to the 2nd, use the 2nd house keywords, and say "my possessions as they relate to my abundance, my earning abilities as they relate to my abundance, my self-esteem as it relates to my abundance," as you look through the cards. Continue this process until you have selected a card for every house. If you feel that you really need to, you can pick more than one card per house, but try to narrow it down as much as you can. Use the following chart to fill in your cards in their houses.

House	Tarot Card	Heavenly Bodies
1st	_____	_____
2nd	_____	_____
3rd	_____	_____

House	Tarot Card	Heavenly Bodies
4th	_____	_____
5th	_____	_____
6th	_____	_____
7th	_____	_____
8th	_____	_____
9th	_____	_____
10th	_____	_____
11th	_____	_____
12th	_____	_____

Next take out your astrological birth chart. Starting with your 1st house, list all the heavenly bodies in that house in the space provided. Include all of your planets, your Nodes ☊ ☋, the asteroids, and Chiron ⚷.

Look over your lists. To get a better visual sense of how the Tarot cards you selected for each house relate to your astrological birth chart, place the cards in a circle around your natal chart so that each card corresponds to its appropriate house. Or, if you feel so inclined, draw your cards in a ring that fits around your birth chart. In a metaphorical sense, the cards are your progressed chart. They represent your Psychic Intuition's sense of where you are now, while your birth chart represents the astrological view of where you were at birth.

Spend some time comparing your Tarot card "progressed chart" to your astrological birth chart. How do the cards that you selected for each house relate to the planets that you have in that house? Spend some time writing about this in your notebook. Then look at the planets in other houses and see how they relate to your cards in aspect.

So you'll have a clearer idea of how all this works, Arlene and Katherine tried this exercise, too. Here are the cards that Arlene selected, along with the planets for each of her houses.

House	Tarot Card	Heavenly Bodies
1st	9 of Wands	Jupiter ♃
2nd	Queen of Wands 3 of Pentacles	None
3rd	Chariot 2 of Wands	Moon ☽

House	Tarot Card	Heavenly Bodies
4th	Ace of Pentacles Knight of Cups	Uranus ♅
5th	Knight of Swords Knight of Wands 9 of Swords R	None
6th	8 of Pentacles 3 of Cups	Pluto ♀ South Node ☋
7th	Hermit Ace of Cups	Saturn ♄ Neptune ♆
8th	Acc of Swords The World	Mars ♂
9th	Page of Wands High Priestess	None
10th	3 of Wands Justice	Venus ♀ Chiron ⚷
11th	Temperance	Mercury ☿
12th	King of Pentacles 6 of Cups King of Cups	Sun ☉ North Node ☊

The first thing we see in Arlene's cards is a focus on Wands and Pentacles. These cards reflect the work Arlene has been doing on her money issues and toward developing her business. The strong sense about her today is to produce and continue to develop herself through her work and career efforts. The 9 of Wands in the 1st house indicates that Arlene feels well prepared to deal with stresses of a work nature and can keep herself focused on developing more abundance. The cards show that Arlene has given herself a personal challenge to create more abundance, and she doesn't need any outside influences to persuade her to take action. Jupiter ♃ in Arlene's natal 1st house adds the needed enthusiasm to continue her forward momentum.

In the 2nd house, the house of finances, the Queen of Wands and the 3 of Pentacles indicate another personal focus on finances. This Queen can represent Arlene herself or a collective of the women around her who cheer her on with her finance and prosperity work. These cards indicate a well-balanced creative flow in this house. Because there are no planets in Arlene's 2nd house, these cards reflect how Arlene has grown to focus on an area of her life that might not have been as much of a focus for her growth until now.

The Moon ☽ in Arlene's 3rd house coupled with the Chariot and the 2 of Wands shows that Arlene's ability to communicate has improved over time. These cards reflect that Arlene feels confident and very intent upon making herself understood in all areas of written, spoken, and mental communication. She has evolved to feel better about her 3rd house issues and the Chariot (overcoming of difficulty) and the 2 of Wands (looking for a response from others) truly reflect how Arlene is today.

Arlene's natal Venus ♀ in the 10th house of career shares its areas with cards that reflect goals of abundance as well. The desire of the 3 of Wands and Justice are to focus outward to the world and fairly do the work that it takes to remain abundant. Arlene's career and public image would be connected to the enthusiasm of the Wands and the ethical and honest intent of Justice. When she saw these cards, Arlene thought, "Yes, I do try to be fair and honest with regard to what the public may need from me." Of course, as a teacher and a professional reader, handling people's problems can be quite intense. So Arlene is always on her toes to stay aware of the needs of both her public and her own career. So far, so good for Arlene's growth and abundance!

It took Katherine longer than she thought it would to find cards for all of her houses. And then she had a hard time narrowing down her selection. She had 12 cards that she liked for her 12th house, but after some deliberation she managed to cut them down to 3. Because she has three planets in her 12th house, this felt like the right number to her. Here are the cards that Katherine picked for each house. She's filled in the planets in each of her houses, as well.

House	Tarot Card	Heavenly Bodies
1st	4 of Cups Page of Swords	None
2nd	The Moon	Jupiter, Saturn ♃, ♄
3rd	7 of Swords	None
4th	Temperance	Chiron, South Node ⚷, ☋
5th	2 of Pentacles	None
6th	Page of Cups	None
7th	7 of Cups	Moon ☽
8th	Ace of Swords	Mars ♂
9th	Knight of Swords	Uranus ♅
10th	8 of Pentacles	Pluto, North Node ♀, ☊
11th	The Hermit	Sun ☉

House	Tarot Card	Heavenly Bodies
12th	Page of Pentacles R	Neptune Ψ
	Queen of Swords	Mercury ☿
	Ace of Pentacles	Venus ♀

The first thing we notice about Katherine's cards is that she chose a lot of Swords. Of her 15 cards, 5 belong to that suit—that's a lot of Air energy! (Remember that Swords is the Tarot suit associated with the element of Air? And 5 is the number of change!) She also picked four Pentacles—the suit of money, abundance, and Earth energy—and three Cups—the suit of emotions, intuition, and Water—and three cards from the Major Arcana. Given Katherine's penchant for double espressos, we were surprised to see that she did not pick a single card from the fiery suit of Wands.

The 4 of Cups and the Page of Swords together in the 1st house would indicate a certain dual nature; Katherine can be removed and indecisive like the 4 of Cups, or vigilant and intent like the Page of Swords with regard to her abundance and the conditions affecting it. Because the Page of Swords is often thought of as the messenger of vigilance, urging us to take a closer look and pay attention, Katherine wonders if this card doesn't speak to her role in the writing of this book about abundance. We were also interested to note that the Page of Swords, which is associated with the planet Mercury ☿, sits opposite Katherine's natal Moon ☽ in the 7th house, which is in Gemini ♊, one of the signs ruled by Mercury. In the 2nd house, the area of possession and earning abilities, the Moon card, which depicts the wild versus the tame, the predictable and in control versus the unpredictable and the out of control, sits with Katherine's natal Jupiter ♃ and Saturn ♄. This also shows a duality connected to money, values, potential for income, and earning capacity. Katherine was struck that Temperance in her 4th house makes a trine △ to her 12th house, and this perhaps shows a soothing of the energy of her three 12th house planets (Venus ♀, Mercury ☿, and Neptune Ψ), which are all in intense Scorpio ♏. We could go on and on about this combined Tarot and Astrology chart! But we think you get the idea.

Because this double chart provides so much information, you may want to keep the cards circled around your birth chart for a while. We've been looking at ours for a couple of days, and each time we come back we notice new and interesting alignments. If you can, tape your cards down in their house positions and make a photocopy of them. Or take a photograph with your digital camera and save the photo on your computer. That way you'll be able to study the relationship between your cards, planets, and houses at your leisure, and you'll have a reminder of your intuitive progression for today.

A Day of Abundance

Now that you've seen your Intuitive Arts chart of where you are in the present in relation to your abundance, you are going to take a look at your goals for the future. You need a quiet place where you can sit and think, some uninterrupted time, your notebook, and a pen. You also need your Tarot deck.

Settle down and make yourself comfortable. Roll your shoulders a little and take a few deep breaths to help you relax. Then close your eyes and start to imagine your ideal day of abundance.

Start your day at the beginning—when you wake up. Where are you? What woke you up? Do you hear anything special? How do the sheets on the bed feel? What does the room you are in look like? Does it have a special scent?

Imagine yourself getting out of bed. Notice the view and the weather from your window. See the room that you enter next. Whether it is the bathroom or the kitchen, fill in all the little details of this room that make it special and that make you feel abundant. Does your space contain plants? Are animals a part of your ideal abundant day? Other people? Children? And what about food and drink?

Continue to imagine your ideal day, step by step, moment by moment, until you reach the end of the day and return to bed. Run through your ideal day in your head as if it were a movie. Add any elements that you like and revise the details until your imagined day is just perfect.

Next record your day in your notebook. If drawing works better than writing for you, go ahead and sketch images of your day. Or use a combination of graphics and words—whatever works for you. It's your ideal day, after all!

Now choose 12 key moments from your ideal day. Circle each one in your notes, and as you do so allow yourself to re-experience the moment you have chosen.

Your next step is to fan out your Tarot cards. You are going to choose 1 card to represent each of the 12 key moments that you selected from your ideal day. Start at the beginning of your day with your first key moment. Close your eyes and focus on how that moment feels. Hold on to that feeling while you leaf through your cards. Keep looking at the cards until you find the one that captures that moment from your ideal day.

Once you have selected 1 card for each of your 12 key moments, take a look at the following diagram.

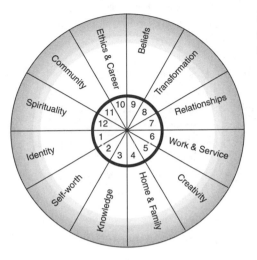

Place each of your key moment cards on the house that feels right to you.

Looks familiar, doesn't it? And you've already guessed what you are going to do next, right? Yup, you are going to place each card you have selected to represent the key moments of your abundant day in the astrological house that feels right to you. To do this, start with your first card, the one that represents the earliest chronological moment in your ideal day of abundance. As you hold the card, visualize the moment that it represents and feel all the abundant details. Then put the card in the appropriate house.

If you want to put more than one card in a given house, go right ahead. Having more than one card in a house just reflects an emphasis on that house, just the way having more than one planet in a house in your natal chart tends to emphasize that area of your life. It's also okay for this exercise if you end up with houses with no cards in them. A cardless house, just like a planetless house in an astrological birth chart, is neither empty nor inactive. If you feel the need, though, go ahead and choose another card to put in a house without any cards in it.

Make a note of the cards in their positions. As a representation of your ideal abundant day, this circle of cards is *where you want to go.* So write the card names on the house chart. Draw them in your note-book. Or tape them down to a sheet of paper and make a color photo-copy or digital photograph of them. Why not hang it in your prosperity corner to remind you of your abundance goals? You'll also want to compare this "card chart," based on your ideal abundant day, with the Tarot card chart that you made in the earlier exercise in this chapter. Try placing your abundant day cards in a circle outside of the cards that you chose to represent you and your abundance in the present day. You can think of these two charts combined as your Psychic Intuition's view of you in the present with your ideal progression—the cards representing your ideal abundant day—on the outside.

Now why not give yourself a taste of your ideal day of abundance? Think of one thing that you can do now to let yourself enjoy a part of your ideal day. Maybe that will mean sleeping late or having blueberries for breakfast—even if they are out of season and cost "too much." Perhaps you can buy yourself fresh flowers, light some incense while you take a bath, or listen to music while you prepare dinner. Pick one thing now and commit to doing it for yourself—because you really are worth it.

Your Abundance Balance Sheet

You've learned a lot about how the Intuitive Arts can help you understand your relationship to money and abundance. You've also seen how you can use Astrology, Tarot, and Psychic Intuition to help you define what you want and begin to work toward getting it. Now you are going to pull together all the information you have gathered on your journey through this book and create your personal Abundance Balance Sheet. We've provided a convenient worksheet so you can compile all of your information into one handy spot. Gathering your data together will allow you to explore the equation of your assets, goals, strengths, and achievements in a fun way. And after you're done you'll have a firm grip on your bottom line.

First look back to Chapter 2 and find your *yin/yang* balance. Do the astrological signs of your financial planets represent mostly *yin* or mostly *yang* energy?

In Chapter 3, you learned about the four Elements—Fire, Water, Air, and Earth—and discovered your Elemental Abundance Signature. Is your Elemental Abundance Signature primarily Fire, Water, Air, or Earth?

And what is your typical Elemental energy? Do you run mostly on Fire, Water, Air, or Earth?

Now you are going to combine the information you ascertained in Chapters 1 through 4. From Chapter 1, record your Sun ☉ sign and house and your rising sign (or ascendant). From Chapter 2, note the astrological sign and house of your financial planets. From Chapter 4, record the house and astrological sign of your Moon ☽.

	Astro Sign	**House**
Sun ☉	_____	_____
Moon ☽	_____	_____
Venus ♀	_____	_____
Mars ♂	_____	_____

	Astro Sign	**House**
Jupiter ♃	_____	_____
Saturn ♄	_____	_____
Ascendant	_____	_____

Now make a note of your Lunar High and Lunar Low.

High: _____

Low: _____

Next, from Chapter 7, note the placements of your outer planets, your asteroids, and Chiron.

Uranus ♅	_____	_____
Neptune ♆	_____	_____
Pluto ♇	_____	_____
Ceres ⚳	_____	_____
Juno ⚵	_____	_____
Pallas Athene ⚴	_____	_____
Vesta ⚶	_____	_____
Chiron ⚷	_____	_____

Now go back over the lists of planets and note if any of your planets show a personal retrograde. Mark any retrograde planet in your birth chart with ℞, the symbol for retrograde.

From Chapter 5, write down any aspects for each of your financial planets.

Venus ♀ _____

Mars ♂ _____

Jupiter ♃ _____

Saturn ♄ _____

Write a few sentences about how these aspects are gifts to you that can enhance your personal abundance.

_____

_____

_____

If you did so in Chapter 5, make a note of the aspects between your financial planets and the planets in your partner's chart.

Venus ♀ _____

Mars ♂ _____

Jupiter ♃ _____

Saturn ♄ _____

In Chapter 6, you read about Saturn returns and Pluto squares. Make a note of your Saturn and your midlife Pluto transit.

Have you experienced your Saturn return?

Yes _____ No, not yet _____

Have you experienced transiting Pluto squaring your natal Pluto?

Yes _____ No, not yet _____

In Chapter 8, you learned that your North Node ☊ reveals your challenges, while your South Node ☋ shows the things that come easily to you. Note down the sign and house for your North Node/South Node pair.

	Astro Sign	**House**
Nodal Pair		
North Node ☊	_____	_____
South Node ☋	_____	_____

Your Nodal challenge: _____

You also looked at your 2nd house in this chapter to see what kind of relationship it has with your Nodes and their challenge.

Your 2nd house sign: _____

Your 2nd house ruler: _____

If you found any significant relationships between your 2nd house, your 2nd house planets, or your 2nd house ruler, make a note of them here.

_____

_____

Take a moment now to review the two charts that you made from Tarot cards earlier in this chapter. Remind yourself that you have the power to pursue your dreams and make your ideal abundant day a reality. With your newfound understanding from Astrology, Tarot, and your Psychic Intuition, you can harness the beneficial energies all around you while avoiding the less-favorable moments to act. So let your Abundance Balance Sheet be a springboard to catapult you into the prosperous future of your dreams.

Staying on the Path to Abundance

After you are done reading this book and have completed all the exercises, then what? How will you keep yourself inspired and keep moving ahead on the path to your own abundance? One thing you can do is read books about the aspects of personal finance that interest you. We particularly like the books of Suze Orman. She's one Gemini ♊ with a sensible message about money and the spirit, which she delivers in an accessible and easily understood way. Check out her website (www.suzeorman.com) for a listing of her titles, and look for her column in Oprah's magazine.

Another thing you can do that we've found quite fun is to maintain your prosperity corner as a special place. Let all the objects in your prosperity corner enhance the energy of abundance in your home. And allow your corner to be a physical reminder of your goals. It is so easy to get swept up into the short-term gratification of impulse buying. Keeping your eyes, heart, and wallet focused on your long-term goals can be tricky, especially when you are bombarded with advertisements that urge you to spend, spend, spend, and spend some more. If you know that you want to save to buy a house or a car, why not post an image of your dream home or vehicle in your prosperity corner? Or post an image that embodies your life as a debt-free individual. Let your prosperity corner images inspire you and remind you. If you can stay clear about your long-term goals, it will be easier to forgo that pair of shoes you saw on sale that you know you don't really need anyhow.

The Empress and the Emperor are among the many Tarot cards that represent abundance.

There are many symbols of abundance that you can use in your prosperity corner or in other places in your home or office. In the eighteenth century, images of pineapples were used as decorations on gateposts to signify wealth and welcome. Pineapples were considered to be so luxurious and expensive that people even rented them at Christmastime to use as the centerpiece for their holiday tables. In the present day, restaurant and business owners often post the first dollar bill that their new enterprise brings in by the cash register to draw in even more dollars. In addition to many of the other cards we have discussed, Tarot's Empress and Emperor, or your rendering of them and their energies, could make a helpful addition to a prosperity corner. Or choose an image of a cornucopia, spilling over with ripe fruit, a symbol of plenty that has been in use for centuries; as have many varieties of fruit—grapes, mangoes, oranges, peaches, pineapples, pomegranates, and tangerines, to name a few. Here's a list to help you think about which symbols of prosperity and abundance resonate for you:

Bears	Fruit
Bells	Honey
Buffalo	Pinecones
Cinnamon	Rabbits
Cloves	Rain clouds
Cornucopia (horn of plenty)	Sheaves of wheat
Cows	Squash blossoms
Ears of corn	Tulips
Frogs	Wine

You can use any image or object in your prosperity corner that says abundance to you—it might be a photograph from a magazine of a pint of blueberries, an image of a pair of shiny red boots, a photo of a tree in full leaf, an actual tree leaf, a piece of jewelry, a drawing of a rainbow and a pot of gold, a piece of velvet, an image of a sunrise, your favorite book, a copy of a poem that you wrote, or a painting from a museum, such as Quentin Metsys's *The Banker and His Wife* (1514), which, in a domestic scene of a man and woman sitting at a table, seems to depict the simultaneous unity and duality of money and spirit—the *yin* and *yang* of your abundance. To see an electronic file of the actual painting, log on to www.louvre.fr/anglais/collec/peint/inv1444/inv1444.htm.

The Banker and His Wife *(1514) by Quentin Metsys seems to capture the spiritual* yin *and* yang *of abundance.*

A Phalanx of Phoenixes

While you are thinking about which symbols of abundance work for you, try something new. Here are directions for how to make a paper Phoenix decoration. This design is based on a traditional Chinese cut-paper pattern. You can use these Phoenixes to draw good things toward you. The Phoenix, you will recall, not only has the ability to rise from the ashes, it can also bring financial luck and prosperity.

You need:

- A square sheet of paper in a color that says "abundance" to you
- Scissors—the smaller and sharper the better—or an Exacto knife
- A sheet of paper in a contrasting color
- A glue stick

1. Fold your paper in half on the diagonal. If you are using paper that is colored on one side and white on the other, such as origami paper, keep the color on the inside when you fold. It's easier to make a precise fold if you turn the paper so one of the corners is pointing toward you. Then make your fold by lifting the corner nearest you. Take it to meet the far corner exactly and form a crease along the paper's diagonal.
2. Fold both bottom points up to meet at the top.
3. Fold the entire figure in half by bringing the left point over to meet the right.
4. Trace the design here onto your paper, then carefully cut it out.

Unfold the paper gently. Then attach your Phoenix decoration to a sheet of paper in a contrasting color and hang it on a wall of your prosperity corner. Alternatively, post it over the computer where you work or display it near the place where you sit to pay your bills, and let the Phoenixes' wings fan you with the energy of abundance.

1) Fold paper in half on the diagonal

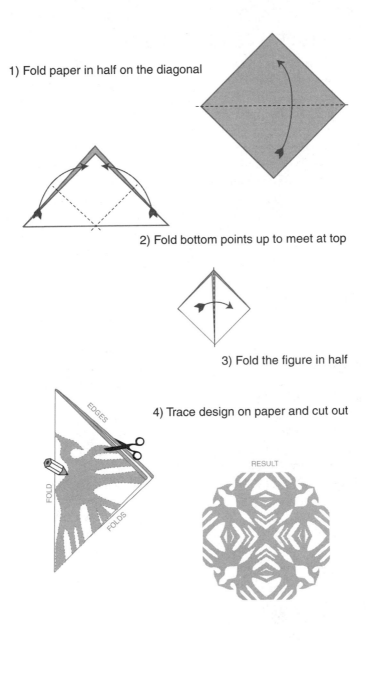

2) Fold bottom points up to meet at top

3) Fold the figure in half

4) Trace design on paper and cut out

RESULT

Hello, Kitty: The Good Fortune Cat

Another one of our favorite symbols of abundance is Maneki Neko, the Japanese good-fortune cat. You've probably seen small statues of this cat in the windows of Asian restaurants and shops. The cat holds one paw up, as if beckoning customers to come in. There are actually a number of varieties of Maneki Neko figures. The cat with its left paw raised is welcoming customers or people to enter a place of business. The cat with its right paw held aloft is drawing money and prosperity toward itself. While the traditional Maneki Neko is white or tortoise shell, the figurines also come in a variety of colors with specific meaning assigned to each hue. In Feng Shui, a golden cat of abundance is often placed in the prosperity corner to enhance abundance. This cat is often a two-sided figure. One side depicts a smiling cat with one paw held up to attract wealth and good fortune, while the other side shows a frowning cat holding a broom, which it uses to banish financial worries and all sorts of trouble.

Maneki Neko often is made in the form of a coin bank. So you could put one in your prosperity corner and use it for loose change. At the end of the month, see how much money you have collected. You could donate this sum to the charity of your choice. Pick one that you feel really needs your funds. As Oprah wrote in the premiere issue of her magazine, "Now I know that you receive from the world what you give to the world." In other words, you get what you give. So why not try giving as a means to increase your personal abundance? Planning your giving can help you to feel even more abundant. You could decide to put aside a certain small amount for your selected charity every day and at the end of the month make your donation.

Maneki Neko, the Japanese good-fortune cat, can welcome customers or attract money, depending on which paw it holds up.

Your Abundance and the World

Can we give you the world? Well, we'd like to, but just as Dorothy in the *Wizard of Oz* has to look within to reach her heart's desire, you have to find your own abundance for yourself. And we know that you can. (Just click your heels together three times ....) The World card represents attainment and self-actualization. Think of this card as Dorothy at the end of the film when she realizes that she has the power to get back to Kansas. Just like you do in terms of your own abundance, Dorothy has had the power to manifest what she wants all along. While Dorothy's return to Kansas occurs at the end of the movie, it is a new beginning for her. She now has the opportunity to live among the people and things that she loves with a sense of appreciation, love, and spiritual abundance. In the same way, let the end of this book be a new beginning for you.

Tarot's World represents attainment and self-actualization.

With your new mastery of the Intuitive Arts of Astrology, Tarot, and Psychic Intuition, you will continue to grow, to prosper, and to create and define your own form of abundance in all areas of your life. We wish you luck, prosperity, opportunity, enjoyment, and most importantly the manifestation of your own personal abundance.

appendix A

Abundance Stars

The Wheel of the Zodiac
Planets in Houses
Signs in Houses
Planet Personalities and Rulers
House Keywords
Elements, Energies, and Qualities
Aspects
Looking for and Finding Your Abundance
Ordering Birth Charts and Synastry Grids Online

We've put together this quick-reference appendix as a guide to under-standing Astrology's signs, planets, and houses. Use this information to aid you in locating abundance in your own birth chart—and developing it in your life, too!

The Wheel of the Zodiac

By the Signs

Here's a quick, handy reference to the astrological signs.

Aries, the Ram ♈	**March 21 to April 20**
Element	Fire
Quality	Cardinal
Energy	*Yang*
Rulers	Mars and Pluto
Anatomy	Brain, eyes, face
Keywords	Pioneering, initiating, beginnings

Taurus, the Bull ♉	**April 20 to May 21**
Element	Earth
Quality	Fixed
Energy	*Yin*
Ruler	Venus
Anatomy	Neck, throat, thyroid
Keywords	Ownership, dependability, sensuality

Gemini, the Twins ♊ May 21 to June 22

Element	Air
Quality	Mutable
Energy	*Yang*
Ruler	Mercury
Anatomy	Hands, arms, shoulders, lungs
Keywords	Mentality, communication, versatility

Cancer, the Crab ♋ June 22 to July 23

Element	Water
Quality	Cardinal
Energy	*Yin*
Ruler	Moon
Anatomy	Stomach, breasts
Keywords	Feeling, sensitivity, nurturing

Leo, the Lion ♌ July 23 to August 22

Element	Fire
Quality	Fixed
Energy	*Yang*
Ruler	Sun
Anatomy	Back, spine, heart
Keywords	Willpower, creativity, expressing the heart

Virgo, the Virgin ♍ August 22 to September 22

Element	Earth
Quality	Mutable
Energy	*Yin*
Ruler	Mercury
Anatomy	Intestines, colon
Keywords	Service, self-improvement, sacred patterns

Libra, the Scales ♎ September 22 to October 23

Element	Air
Quality	Cardinal
Energy	*Yang*
Ruler	Venus
Anatomy	Kidneys, lower back, adrenal glands
Keywords	Balance, harmony, justice

Scorpio, the Scorpion ♏   October 23 to November 22

Element	Water
Quality	Fixed
Energy	*Yin*
Rulers	Pluto and Mars
Anatomy	Genitals, urinary and reproductive systems
Keywords	Desire, transformation, power

Sagittarius, the Archer ♐   November 22 to December 22

Element	Fire
Quality	Mutable
Energy	*Yang*
Ruler	Jupiter
Anatomy	Liver, hips, thighs
Keywords	Understanding, enthusiasm, exploration

Capricorn, the Goat ♑   December 22 to January 21

Element	Earth
Quality	Cardinal
Energy	*Yin*
Ruler	Saturn
Anatomy	Bones, joints, knees, teeth
Keywords	Achievement, structure, organization

Aquarius, the Water Bearer ♒   January 21 to February 19

Element	Air
Quality	Fixed
Energy	*Yang*
Rulers	Uranus and Saturn
Anatomy	Ankles, circulation
Keywords	Humanitarian, unique, innovative

Pisces, the Fishes ♓   February 19 to March 21

Element	Water
Quality	Mutable
Energy	*Yin*

Pisces, the Fishes ♓   **February 19 to March 21**

Rulers	Neptune and Jupiter
Anatomy	Feet, immune system, hormonal system
Keywords	Compassion, universality, inclusiveness

By the Planets

Here's a quick, handy reference to the energy of each planet.

Planet	Symbol	Energies	Action Keyword
Sun	☉	Self, essence, life spirit, creativity, willpower	Explores
Moon	☽	Emotions, instincts, unconscious, past memories	Senses
Mercury	☿	Mental activities, communication, intelligence	Communicates
Venus	♀	Love, art, beauty, social graces, harmony, money, resources, possessions	Enjoys
Mars	♂	Physical energy, boldness, warrior ways, action, desires anger, courage, ego	Acts
Jupiter	♃	Luck, abundance, wisdom, higher education, philosophy or beliefs, exploration, growth	Benefits
Saturn	♄	Responsibilities, self-discipline, perseverance, limitations, structures	Works
Uranus	♅	Sudden or unexpected change, originality, liberation, radical thinking, authenticity	Innovates
Neptune	♆	Idealism, subconscious, spirituality, intuition, clairvoyance	Dreams
Pluto	♇	Power, regeneration, destruction, rebirth, transformation	Transforms

Signs in Houses

House	Astro Sign
1st	Aries ♈
2nd	Taurus ♉
3rd	Gemini ♊
4th	Cancer ♋
5th	Leo ♌
6th	Virgo ♍
7th	Libra ♎
8th	Scorpio ♏
9th	Sagittarius ♐
10th	Capricorn ♑
11th	Aquarius ♒
12th	Pisces ♓

Planetary Rulers

Planet	Signs Ruled
Sun ☉	Leo ♌
Moon ☽	Cancer ♋
Mercury ☿	Gemini ♊, Virgo ♍
Venus ♀	Taurus ♉, Libra ♎
Mars ♂	Aries ♈, co-ruler of Scorpio ♏
Jupiter ♃	Sagittarius ♐, co-ruler of Pisces ♓
Saturn ♄	Capricorn ♑, co-ruler of Aquarius ♒
Uranus ♅	Aquarius ♒
Neptune ♆	Pisces ♓
Pluto ♇	Scorpio ♏, co-ruler of Aries ♈

House Key Terms

House	Key Term
1st	Identity
2nd	Self-worth
3rd	Knowledge
4th	Home and family
5th	Creativity
6th	Work and service
7th	Relationships

House	Key Term
8th	Transformation
9th	Beliefs
10th	Ethics and career
11th	Community
12th	Spirituality

Natural Planets and Natural Signs in Their Houses

Here are the natural planets and natural signs in their astrological houses.

Asteroids and Planetoids

More than just the planets move through your birth chart! Here are the asteroids and the planetoid Chiron, and their areas of influence.

Asteroid	Realm	Areas of Influence
Ceres ?	Motherhood	Natural cycles, fertility, crops, relationships between parents and children
Juno ⚹	Marriage	Partnerships, contracts and agreements, social obligations
Pallas Athene ⚴	Wisdom	Intelligence, knowledge, understanding, equality
Vesta ⚶	Power	Sexuality, devotion, health, service to others
Planetoid		
Chiron ⚷	Healing	Transformation, personal growth

Astrological Extras

The astrological charts and grids you see as examples throughout this book contain two symbols we don't include in our discussions but that might interest you in your further explorations of Astrology. These are the Part of Fortune ⊗ and the minor asteroid Lilith ⚸. The Part of Fortune, sometimes called the Lot of Fortune, derives from ancient Astrology and represents the intersection in the Zodiac where your Sun ☉, Moon ☽, and ascendant converge. The Part of Fortune in its basic symbolism is a "point of karmic reward" in your birth chart. The ancients believed the Part of Fortune is what you would receive as a cosmic gift as you grew in this lifetime. Lilith, also called the Dark Moon, represents primal and emotional connections to your shadow side, and "liberation from conformity" in present day interpretations.

Aspects

Aspects are the geometric relationships between any two planets in your own chart, as well as in relation to another chart, whether for another person, a moment in time, or your own progressed chart. The main aspects to consider are the following:

- ☽ **Conjunction** ☌   The strongest aspects. In a conjunction, the planets are placed at the same point in a chart or charts. Conjunctions are considered a focal point, with the interaction of the two planets emphasized.

- **Sextile** ✷ In a sextile, the planets are 60° apart. The signs in a sextile share the same energy (*yin* or *yang*), so this is considered to be a favorable aspect.
- **Square** □ In a square, the planets are 90° apart. While squares are considered to be chart challenges, they often provide the impetus for change and improvement.
- **Trine** △ In a trine, the planets are 120° apart. This most favorable of the aspects means the planets share both element and energy. Trines indicate positive connections, often made so easily you may not even notice.
- **Opposition** ☍ In an opposition, the planets are 180° apart. There's little in common with an opposition, but, like squares, their difficult energy can spur us on to meet challenges.
- **Quincunx** ⚻ In a quincunx, the planets are 150° apart. Quincunxes are interesting—nothing is shared between the two signs, so some adjustment is usually required for them to interact.

Looking for and Finding Your Abundance

Money and abundance are everywhere on your birth chart, but there are a few special places that will give you a quick financial assessment. We've used Warren Buffett's birth chart and numbered the areas to pay special attention to when you're looking for your own personal abundance. We've also cross-referenced the chapters that cover this area in detail.

1. In Chapter 1, we showed you where to look for your Sun ☉, the planet in your chart that represents you, and your ascendant or rising sign, which describes the face that you show to the world and the way that you express yourself.
2. In Chapter 2, you learned about your *yin/yang* equation: which planets in your chart sit in signs with a *yin* quality and which have a *yang* quality.
3. In Chapter 3, we introduced you to your Elemental Abundance Signature, how many financial planets you have in Fire, Earth, Air, and Water signs.
4. In Chapter 4, you learned how the Moon ☽ as it travels through the signs and through its phases can impact you and your financial dealings. You also learned how to determine which days in

the month are your Lunar High, the days when the energy of Moon's ☽ sign will give you a boost.

5. In Chapter 5, we introduced you to synastry, and showed you how to use an aspect grid to see how the planets in your chart relate to one another around money issues. You also saw how to use an aspect grid to get a sense of how a relationship with another person can impact your money and abundance and vice versa.

6. In Chapter 6, we looked at Saturn ♄ returns, and Pluto ♀ transits, so that you could find times when your birth chart might be generating personal financial change.

7. In Chapter 7, you learned about retrogrades ℞, a planetary cycle that affects everyone, and how these celestial movements can affect your abundance.

   Also in Chapter 7, we introduced you to the asteroids—Ceres ⚵, Juno ⚵, Pallas Athene ⚴, and Vesta ⚶—and showed you how these heavenly bodies can impact your life and your livelihood. In addition, we introduced you to Chiron ⚷, a recently discovered asteroid.

8. In Chapter 8, you learned how the North ☊ and South Node ☋ describe your challenge and how aspects between Venus ♀, your Nodes, and your second house ruler can refine and further specify what kind of karma you have in relation to abundance.

9. Finally in Chapter 9, you looked at transits, progressions, and a very successful event chart. You learned that you can use astrology to plan and help to make all of your financial events successful steps on the path toward your personal abundance.

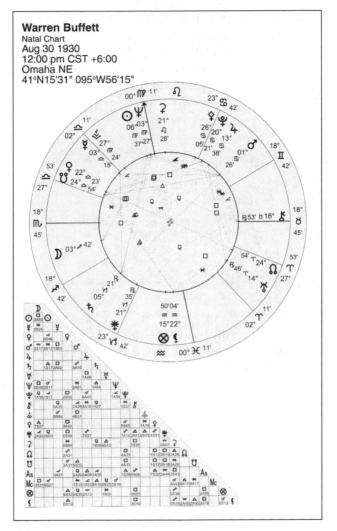

Warren Buffett's birth chart and aspect grid.

Ordering Birth Charts and Synastry Grids Online

Several websites will prepare birth charts for you. To get a birth chart you can use with this book, be sure to specify Geocentric, Tropical Zodiac, Placidus house system, and True Node. Check out Arlene's site at www.mellinetti.com. Also check out Astrolabe, Inc., at www.alabe. com.

This is the company that publishes Solar Fire, the computer software program Arlene used to generate the birth charts we used as examples throughout this book. A few other good Astrology websites include www.astro.com, www.astrodatabank.com, and www.stariq. com. There are many astrological sites on the Internet; explore and choose the site that resonates for you and your investigation of Astrology, the heavens, and your abundant place in the universe.

Birth Time and Your Birth Chart

The position of the Sun ☉ in the heavens at the time of your birth determines the placement of the planets and signs in the houses of your astrological birth chart. To know the precise position of the Sun, you need to know the location, date, and time of your birth. Many people don't know their birth times. There are various methods astrologers can use to cast birth charts when this is the case.

For the birth charts with unknown birth times that we used in this book, Arlene used the method called "noon chart." A noon chart uses noon as your time of birth, placing your Sun ☉ at the apex of the horoscope wheel—on your midheaven. Symbolically, this puts your soul at its highest potential in this lifetime, looking down with an eagle-eye view, so to speak, on the planets and how they "fall" into place in the astrological houses to represent your life. Although there is some imprecision with this or any method of casting a birth chart without a precise time of birth (for example, the ascendant sign changes every two hours), Arlene finds the noon chart allows the most accurate interpretations for the broadest range of people.

Abundance Cards

Because Tarot is a tool that helps you use your Psychic Intuition to read the energies around you, or around another person, no Tarot card's meaning is absolute. For that reason, we encourage you to make your own personal interpretations of the cards. You will want to both study the cards' individual images and examine the stories the cards create when read together. These images are from the Universal Waite Tarot Deck published by U.S. Games Systems, Inc.

Besides the personal nature of each card's meaning, you will want to be aware of the traditional interpretation of the cards as well. The traditional meaning can often give you a different perspective that you might not have considered in your initial interpretation. Here you will find the cards' meanings as they apply specifically to your abundance.

Tarot's Major Arcana

The Fool
New opportunity
Endless
possibilities
Innocence and
optimism

The Fool R
Uncertainty
and delays
A wrong direction
Look before you
leap!

The Magician
The power to
manifest desire
Ask and you
shall receive
A creative or
inventive person

The Magician R
Unused talent
or skills
Lack of follow-
through
Possibility of
manipulation

The High Priestess
Intuition and
inner knowing
Yin and yang—
emotions + logic
Going with
your gut

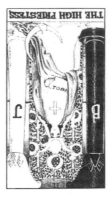

The High Priestess R
Dream or illusion
A hidden agenda
Lack of insight

The Empress
Growth and
prosperity
Happiness to
come
A peaceful and
abundant home

The Empress R
Lack of security
Too much focus
on physical
appearance
Conflict at home

The Emperor
Leadership
Logic
Past experience
can guide the
present

The Emperor R
Insecurity
Stubbornness
Plan first, then act

The Hierophant
Traditional plan-
ning
Staying between
the lines
A solid spiritual
foundation

The Hierophant R
An unconventional
approach to
resources
A risk-taker
Nontraditional
business

The Lovers
Abundant choices
Good start for
a relationship
or project
Peaceful coexis-
tence

The Lovers R
Obstacles to desires
Indecision
An unsatisfying
choice

*The Chariot
Ability to meet
challenges
Focus and deter-
mination to
achieve goal
Positive outcome
after difficult
time*

*The Chariot R
Confusion
Someone else in
control
A battle not
worth fighting?*

*Strength
The inner strength
that comes
from love
Calmness and
compassion
The power of
gentle persuasion*

*Strength R
A power struggle
Intense emotions
that can lead
to upset
Uncontrolled
passions*

*The Hermit
Introspection and
solitude
A desire for truth
Trust own inner
voice for guid-
ance*

*The Hermit R
Inability to
see clearly
Wishing instead
of acting
A reminder to
pay attention to
past lessons*

*The Wheel of
Fortune
Destiny comes
calling!
Luck
Financial or busi-
ness opportunity*

*The Wheel of
Fortune R
What goes up must
come down
Lack of progress
and stagnation
A grinding halt*

*Justice
Fairness and a
desire for balance
A legal agreement
Universal laws
will prevail*

*Justice R
Unwise counsel
Conditions that
are out of balance
Too much subjec-
tivity*

*The Hanged Man
Desire for a dif-
ferent lifestyle
Need to reflect
on the past
A lack of
motion—feeling
"stuck"*

*The Hanged Man R
Difficulty in giving
up old lifestyle
Inability to feel
present abundance
Fear of change*

Death
*The end of an
old pattern
makes way
for new
A catalyst for
change
A new dawn*

*Death R
Past blockages
impede progress
Stagnation and
stalemate
Conflicts; too
tired to care*

*Temperance
A balance
between emotion
and desire
Giving and taking
in equal measure
The importance
of moderation*

*Temperance R
Impatience
Inability to listen
to business
partners
Pushiness instead
of patience*

*The Devil
Obsession with
material goods
Addictive
behaviors
Wrong applica-
tion of force,
aggression*

*The Devil R
Freedom from
fear
Ability to unlock
own chains
A burden lifted*

The Tower
Surprise!
Collapse of a
faulty foundation
Don't depend too
much on man-
made things

The Tower R
A surprising nuance
to a situation
Pay attention to
intuitive nudges
Renewed faith after
difficult life change

The Star
A faith in the
abundance of the
universe
Wishes granted
Return of hope

The Star R
Insecurity
Not receiving as
much as you give
A feeling of
loss—not always
warranted

The Moon
Emotions at
full force
A reminder to
trust your psychic
intuition
Unforeseen
changes

The Moon R
Imagination
combined with
good sense
Clarity of light
after darkness
Relief after worry

*The Sun
Personal
contentment
Sunny outlook
for partnerships
Pleasure and
enjoyment*

*The Sun R
Partnership
problems
A need for
professional
guidance
Cloudy forecast*

*Judgement
A new under-
standing of
past lessons
"I can see
clearly now!"
An awakening to
cosmic awareness*

*Judgement R
At a crossroads
Fears holding
you back
Frustrating delays*

*The World
Successful
culmination
Your new life-
style is ready!
Freedom to do
as you desire*

*The World R
A bit more work
is needed to
achieve goal
Life is what
you make it
You're almost
there!*

Tarot's Minor Arcana

Just the way the Major Arcana has an order—moving from the new-ness and innocence of The Fool to the achievement and worldliness of The World—the suits of the Minor Arcana also have a typical order. Usually you will see Wands first, followed by Cups, then Swords, and finally Pentacles, the suit of the physical plane. Because the focus of this book is abundance and the material world, you will find Pentacles listed first.

Pentacles are associated with the element Earth and the signs Taurus ♉, Virgo ♍, and Capricorn ♑. Pentacles represent possessions, money, and the physical world.

Ace of Pentacles
The beginning
of prosperity,
wealth, and
new business
Good common
sense
Happiness of
solid foundation

Ace of Pentacles R
Frustration and
delays
Need to hold tight
to what you have
Need to reassess
priorities

2 of Pentacles
Juggling more
than one thing
Confidence
despite stress
Balance is essen-
tial

2 of Pentacles R
A hard time deciding
something
Need to simplify;
let something go
Need for caution

3 of Pentacles
A time to learn
new things
Approval for
work and talent
An award or
honor

3 of Pentacles R
The reality
doesn't look
like the plan
Lack of
enthusiasm
Sloppy work-
manship

4 of Pentacles
Holding tight to
what you have
Conservative
about money
A miserly person

4 of Pentacles R
Spending more
than you have
Use caution when
spending
Generosity; over-
generosity

5 of Pentacles
A deep sense of
personal loss
Feelings of
separation
Having nowhere
to go

5 of Pentacles R
Renewed hope and
optimism after loss
Negative cycle ends
Can now reap what
was sown

6 of Pentacles
Extra help is
offered
Sharing with
others
Financial reward;
a new job

6 of Pentacles R
Be cautious of
what others offer
More giving
than taking
Bribery and
chicanery

7 of Pentacles
Self-confidence
Payment for
your skill
Financial inde-
pendence

7 of Pentacles R
Poor speculation
Problems with
land or real estate
A need for caution
when speculating

8 of Pentacles
Social approval
Development of
greater skill
Recognition for
job well done

8 of Pentacles R
Delayed production
Lack of balance in
personal life
Someone's burning
out

9 of Pentacles
The comforts
of home
Self-sufficiency
and independence
Prosperity to
share

9 of Pentacles R
Financial
insecurity
Shaken founda-
tions
Uncertainty
about future

10 of Pentacles
The height of
familial security
Assured future
security
A stable and
secure maturity

10 of Pentacles R
Family feud!
Family wealth
at risk
Be cautious with
investments

Page of Pentacles
An eager learner
A message of
happiness
Good news
good results

Page of Pentacles R
A selfish or
demanding child
or person
Differing values
Prejudice or
rebellion

*Knight of Pentacles
Slow and steady
wins the race
Development of
prosperous future
Wise counsel and
good stewardship*

*Knight of Pentacles R
Discontent with
present work
Work slowdowns
Trying to keep up
with the Joneses*

*Queen of Pentacles
A kind, gentle
person
The Earth Mother
personified
A good business
woman or person*

*Queen of Pentacles R
A needy or dependent
person
A lack of confidence
Losses in the home*

*King of Pentacles
A prosperous
businessman
Assured prosperity
Someone who will
share the wealth*

*King of Pentacles R
Laziness or lack of
motivation
Ill-equipped for
financial success
Disorganization, dis-
content about money*

Wands are associated with the element Fire and the signs Aries ♈, Leo ♌, and Sagittarius ♐. Wands represent beginnings and action.

Ace of Wands
A fresh start
The first step
toward creating
your abundance
A new job, proj-
ect, or attitude

Ace of Wands R
Overenthusiasm
gets in your way
Delays or frustration
Pushiness or aggres-
sion

2 of Wands
Waiting for results
A good perspective
A positive attitude

2 of Wands R
Lack of follow-
through
Delays because
of others
A hidden agenda

3 of Wands
Cooperation and
partnership
Good results
forthcoming
Competition

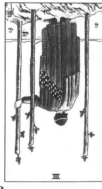

3 of Wands R
Wasted energy
Inadequate
resources
No one in the lead

4 of Wands
Celebration after
hard work
Happiness and
success
A dream come
true

4 of Wands R
Life's little joys
A gathering of
family
Enjoyment of
small pleasures

5 of Wands
Stress and disor-
ganization
Disagreement
and crossed
purposes
Aggression
and misplaced
energies

5 of Wands R
A win-win situation
Compromise and
conciliation
Negotiation and
constructive talks

6 of Wands
Good news
comes home
A happy journey
Success after
troubles

6 of Wands R
Stressful conditions
Need to ride out
the storm
Just not your day

7 of Wands
Anxiety and cau-
tiousness needed
A good offense is
the best defense
Need to face
fears and turn
them around

7 of Wands R
The storm is
passing
A sense of personal
empowerment
Difficulties are over

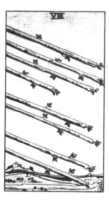

8 of Wands
Success with
current goals
Shared
enthusiasm
Common goals
and ideals

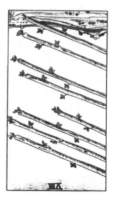

8 of Wands R
Disagreement and
discontent
Anger, jealousy,
or envy
Time to slow down
and reorganize

9 of Wands
Safeguarding
your assets
Forewarned is
forearmed
Well prepared to
handle crisis

9 of Wands R
Vulnerable and tired
Desire to be left
alone
Anxiety and poor
health

10 of Wands
Helping too
many others
at once
Stressful condi-
tions at home or
work
Overwhelming
obligations

10 of Wands R
Shifting the burden
Learning to delegate
Taking the right
approach to respon-
sibility

Page of Wands
An exciting
message
An encouraging
companion
Good tidings arrive

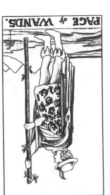

Page of Wands R
Disappointing news
Delay in receiving
expected information
A preoccupied young
person

Knight of Wands
Enthusiasm and
renewed energy
A new adventure
A generous friend
or associate

Knight of Wands R
Postponed journey
Jealousy, arrogance,
or self-doubt
Disorganization or
chaos at the office

*Queen of Wands
In command of
all aspects of
abundance
Someone who
encourages others'
self-sufficiency
Feminine ambition*

*Queen of Wands R
Discomfort on
the home front
Possessive and
domineering
behavior
Confusion and
obstinacy*

*King of Wands
Someone willing
to lend a helping
hand
A good man to
have around in
a crisis
A passionate
mentor*

*King of Wands R
Lack of confidence
Feeling grumpy
and detached
Pessimism or
doubt*

Cups are associated with the element Water and the signs Cancer ♋, Scorpio ♏, and Pisces ♓. Cups represent emotion and intuition.

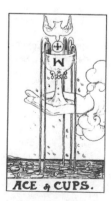

*Ace of Cups
New direction of
the heart
Desire to experi-
ence love and joy
Opening to
spiritual under-
standing*

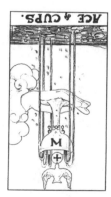

*Ace of Cups R
Insecurity
Inability to con-
nect with others
Too much focus
on self*

2 of Cups
Mutual under-
standing
Good partnership
Sharing of good
ideas

2 of Cups R
Need for cooperation
Negative emotions
Jealousy or posses-
siveness

3 of Cups
Bounty of
the harvest
Happiness all
around
Cause for
celebration

3 of Cups R
Unhappiness
not being com-
municated
Pettiness,
overindulgence
Need to check
emotions

4 of Cups
Detachment
Fantasy more
interesting than
reality
Search for the
spiritual dimen-
sion

4 of Cups R
Ready to try
something new
Ready to recon-
nect with others
Ability to visual-
ize and create
goals and dreams

5 of Cups
Loss
It's okay to cry
Disillusionment,
regrets, broken
dreams

5 of Cups R
Return of posi-
tive energy
and hope
Letting go of
negativity
A new job or
beneficial change
of plans

6 of Cups
Nostalgia for
the old
A past friend
or love returns
bearing gifts
Helpful connec-
tions from the
past

6 of Cups R
Hurtful past situ-
ation has current
echoes
Rewards or
inheritance
delayed
Living in the past
instead of the
present

7 of Cups
Too many
choices!
Pay attention to
what's beneath
Indecisiveness

7 of Cups R
The fog has lifted
A plan has
been made
You finally took
action!

8 of Cups
Surrender to a
higher calling
Leaving the
past behind
Dissatisfaction
with current life

8 of Cups R
Renewed interest
in the material
world
Time to follow
your bliss
Taking pleasure
in life's good
things

9 of Cups
Happy days are
here!
Your wish will
come true
Material success
and security

9 of Cups R
Overindulgence in
good things
Wishes postponed
A need to develop
patience

10 of Cups
Happily ever after!
Joy and happiness
in abundance
Buying a new
home

10 of Cups R
Happiness post-
poned
Damage to home
or reputation
Delays; patience
is needed

Page of Cups
Kindness and
compassion
Someone
who cares
An offer of
happiness

Page of Cups R
Good news delayed
Plans gone awry
Someone who's
oversensitive

Knight of Cups
Movement
toward a heart-
centered goal
An invitation
or proposal
Action toward
developing

Knight of Cups R
Fear of involvement
or commitment
Emotionally
unable to give
Living in a past
relationship

Queen of Cups
A nurturing,
caring person
A focus on feel-
ings, sensitivity,
and intuition
Someone con-
cerned with
others

Queen of Cups R
Someone who
exaggerates feelings
Tendency toward
secrecy or self-
deception
A worrier; an over-
active imagination

King of Cups
A giving, caring person
Someone who understands others
A desire to help others

King of Cups R
A recent emotional loss
Hidden emotions
Potential for manipulation of feelings

Swords are associated with the element Air and the signs Gemini ♊, Libra ♎, and Aquarius ♒. Swords represent communication and mental activity.

Ace of Swords
A new situation
A new way of thinking or communicating
A sword can cut two ways

Ace of Swords R
The need to be cautious and vigilant
Beware of aggression or force
Listen before acting

2 of Swords
Disconnected from emotions
Indecision or stalemate
Need to concentrate and focus

2 of Swords R
Remember to connect to intuition
Use caution to maintain balance
Freedom to make own decisions

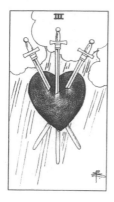

3 of Swords
Sorrow and
disappointment
Fighting among
friends or partners
Learning about
loss and sadness

3 of Swords R
Passing sadness
Dissatisfaction,
but all is not lost
A different result
than what was
expected

4 of Swords
R & R required!
Need for retreat
and meditation
Inner work being
done

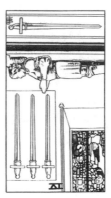

4 of Swords R
Ready for renewed
action
Ready to fight for
own rights
Opportunity to
change existing
condition

5 of Swords
Stormy weather
Someone taking
unfair advantage
Loss, possible
slander

5 of Swords R
Feeling too
weak to fight
Someone being
sneaky
The truth, however
difficult, will out

6 of Swords
Moving away
from sorrow or
difficulty
Acceptance of
better things
to come
Leaving regrets
behind

6 of Swords R
Stuck in a difficult
situation
Better to wait
and see
Learn to be patient

7 of Swords
Someone's being
sneaky
A need for the
truth to come out
Contradictions
and duality

7 of Swords R
Wise counsel
will return
What was hidden
will be revealed
Freedom to
move on

8 of Swords
Self-bound
to fears
Abuse of mental
power
Are you hurting
yourself the
most?

8 of Swords R
Letting go of fear
Facing one's own
restrictions
Ability to move
about freely once
more

9 of Swords
Anxiety, sadness,
and sleeplessness
Learning to deal
with loss and
regret
Emotional
depression

9 of Swords R
The nightmare
is over
Negative energy is
dissipating now
The light at the
end of the tunnel

10 of Swords
End of a karmic
patter
End of a difficult
job
Deep sense of
loss or separation

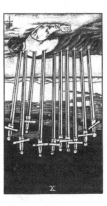

10 of Swords R
Releasing of a
karmic debt
Prepared to
move ahead
End of long,
stressful cycle

Page of Swords
Courage when
needed most
Using common-
sense approach
Pay attention to
details

Page of Swords R
Strange twist of fate
with good results
Need to speak mind
Importance of truth

Knight of Swords
Sudden change of
direction
Direct honesty—
sometimes
too direct
Awakening to
truth

Knight of Swords R
Out of control!
Arguments and dis-
ruptive behavior
Lack of mental
energy

Queen of Swords
Ability to get to
heart of matter
Joy of debate
Honesty and
forthrightness

Queen of Swords R
Overly critical
person
Anxiety and mis-
communication
Judgmental or con-
tentious behavior

King of Swords
Logical analysis
Ability to probe
beneath surface
Rational counsel

King of Swords R
Preconceptions
without basis
Stubbornness and
unfair judgment
Selfishness or
aloofness

About the Authors

Arlene Tognetti grew up in a home where religion and spiritual ideas came together. Her mother, a traditional Catholic, and her father, a more Edgar Cayce–type individual, helped her to understand that there's more to this world than what's obvious. Arlene began studying the Tarot and Astrology in the 1970s and started her own practice in 1980. She began teaching the Tarot at the University of Washington in the Experimental College in 1982, and currently teaches the Tarot at Pierce College in Tacoma. Arlene's focus is on enlightening her students and clients: "I want everyone to learn what Tarot, Astrology, and Psychic Intuition are all about and how these Intuitive Arts can help them grow and look at the choices and alternatives in their lives." Arlene is expert author, with Lisa Lenard, of *The Complete Idiot's Guide to Tarot, Second Edition*. Arlene lives in the Seattle area. Her website is www.mellinetti.com.

Katherine A. Gleason is a freelance writer and editor. She is co-author, with Denise Zimmermann, of the best-selling *The Complete Idiot's Guide to Wicca and Witchcraft, Second Edition,* and with Gail Carr Feldman, Ph.D., of *Releasing the Goddess Within*. Katherine is the author of *Ancient World: A Chapter Book* and numerous other titles for children and young adults. Katherine lives in New York City.

Amaranth Illuminare is a leading book producer, developing New Age and holistic wellness books for mainstream readers. Amaranth's goal: Touch readers' lives. In addition to *The Intuitive Arts* series, Amaranth has developed many books, including *Empowering Your Life with Joy* by Gary McClain, Ph.D., and Eve Adamson; *Thyroid Balance* by Glenn Rothfeld, M.D., and Deborah S. Romaine; and *Menu for Life: African Americans Get Healthy, Eat Well, Lose Weight, and Live Beautifully* by Otelio Randall, M.D., and Donna Randall. Amaranth's founder and creative director, Lee Ann Chearney, is the author of *Visits: Caring for an Aging Parent* and editor of *The Quotable Angel*.

The Intuitive Arts series

Use Astrology, Tarot, and
Psychic Intuition to See Your Future

Discover how you can combine the Intuitive Arts to find answers to
questions of daily living, use tools to help you see and make changes in
your future, claim your brightest destiny, and fulfill your essential nature.

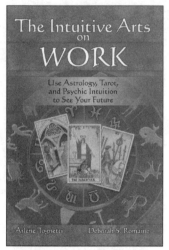

1-59257-108-5

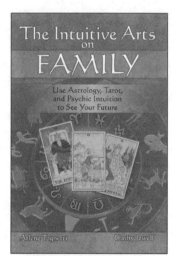

ISBN: 1-59257-110-7

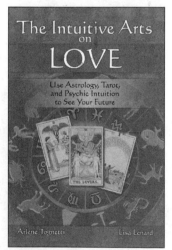

ISBN: 1-59257-106-9

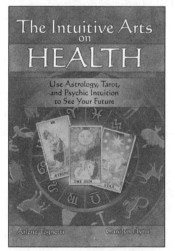

ISBN: 1-59257-109-3

A
ALPHA
A member of Penguin Group (USA) Inc.